SYRACUSE PUBLIC LIBRARY
115 E. MAIN ST
SYRACUSE, IN 46567

DATE DUE

DE 12 '92			

Demco, Inc. 38-293

The
War of 1812

Books in the America's Wars Series:

The Revolutionary War

The Indian Wars

The War of 1812

The Mexican-American War

The Civil War

The Spanish-American War

World War I

World War II: The War in the Pacific

World War II: The War in Europe

The Korean War

The Vietnam War

The Persian Gulf War

The
War of 1812

by Don Nardo

Lucent Books, P.O. Box 289011, San Diego, CA 92198-0011

Library of Congress Cataloging-in-Publication Data

Nardo, Don, 1947–
   The War of 1812/by Don Nardo
        p.   cm.— (America's wars)
   Includes bibliographical references and index
   Summary: An account of the strategies, personalities, and results
of America's second military conflict with Great Britain, the
"unnecessary" and "impractical" War of 1812.
      ISBN 1-56006-401-3
      1. United States—History—War of 1812—Juvenile literature.
   [1. United States—History—War of 1812.]   I. Title.   II. Series.
   E354.N37 1991
   973.5'2—dc20   91-29501
                                                                       CIP
                                                                        AC

Contents

Foreword

War, justifiable or not, is a descent into madness. George Washington, America's first president and commander-in-chief of its armed forces, wrote that his most fervent wish was "to see this plague of mankind, war, banished from the earth." Most, if not all of the forty presidents who succeeded Washington have echoed similar sentiments. Despite this, not one generation of Americans since the founding of the republic has been spared the maelstrom of war. In its brief history of just over two hundred years, the United States has been a combatant in eleven major wars. And four of those conflicts have occurred in the last fifty years.

America's reasons for going to war have differed little from those of most nations. Political, social, and economic forces were at work which either singly or in combination ushered America into each of its wars. A desire for independence motivated the Revolutionary War. The fear of annihilation led to the War of 1812. A related fear, that of having the nation divided, precipitated the Civil War. The need to contain an aggressor nation brought the United States into the Korean War. And territorial ambition lay behind the Mexican-American and the Indian Wars. Like all countries, America, at different times in its history, has been victimized by these forces and its citizens have been called to arms.

Whatever reasons may have been given to justify the use of military force, not all of America's wars have been popular. From the Revolutionary War to the Vietnam War, support of the people has alternately waxed and waned. For example, less than half of the colonists backed America's war of independence. In fact, most historians agree that at least one-third were committed to maintaining America's colonial status. During the Spanish-American War, a strong antiwar movement also developed. Resistance to the war was so high that the Democratic party made condemning the war a significant part of its platform in an attempt to lure voters into voting Democratic. The platform stated that "the burning issue of imperialism growing out of the Spanish war involves the very existence of the Republic and the destruction of our free institutions." More recently, the Vietnam War divided the nation like no other conflict had since the Civil War. The mushrooming antiwar movements in most major cities and colleges throughout the United States did more to bring that war to a conclusion than did actions on the battlefield.

Yet, there have been wars which have enjoyed overwhelming public support. World Wars I and II were popular because people believed that the survival of America's democratic institutions was at stake. In both wars, the American people rallied with an enthusiasm and spirit of self-sacrifice that was remarkable for a country with such a diverse population. Support for food and fuel rationing, the purchase of war bonds, a high rate of voluntary enlistments, and countless other forms of voluntarism, were characteristic of the people's response to those wars. Most recently, the Persian Gulf War prompted an unprecedented show of support even though the United States was not directly threatened by the conflict. Rallies in support of U.S. troops were widespread. Tens of thousands of individuals, including families, friends, and well-wishers of the troops sent packages of food, cosmetics, clothes, cassettes, and suntan oil. And even more supporters wrote letters to unknown soldiers that were forwarded to the military front. In fact, most public opinion polls revealed that up to 90 percent of all Americans approved of their nation's involvement.

The complex interplay of events and purposes that leads to military conflict should be included in a history of any war. A simple chronicling of battles and casualty lists at best offers only a partial history of war. Wars do not spontaneously erupt; nor does their memory perish. They are driven by underlying causes, fueled by policymakers, fought and supported by citizens, and remembered by those plotting a nation's future. For these reasons wars, or the fear of wars, will always leave an indelible stamp on any nation's history and influence its future.

The purpose of this series is to provide a full understanding of America's Wars by presenting each war in a historical context. Each of the twelve volumes focuses on the events that led up to the war, the war itself, its impact on the home front, and its aftermath and influence upon future conflicts. The unique personalities, the dramatic acts of courage and compassion, as well as the despair and horror of war are all presented in this series. Together, they show why America's wars have dominated American consciousness in the past as well as how they guide many political decisions of today. In these vivid and objective accounts, students will gain an understanding of why America became involved in these conflicts, and how historians, military and government officials, and others have come to understand and interpret that involvement.

Chronology of Events

1776
United States declares its independence.

1783
United States wins its independence from Great Britain.

1789
U. S. Constitution is ratified.

1793
War breaks out between Britain and France.

1803
Thomas Jefferson buys the Louisiana Territory from France.

1807
Britain establishes the Orders in Council, restricting American shipping.

British board the USS *Chesapeake* and force U.S. sailors into service.

Congress passes the Embargo Act, cutting off trade with Britain.

1811
William Henry Harrison defeats Indians at Tippecanoe Creek.

1812
June 18   United States declares war on Britain.

July 16–19   USS *Constitution* outruns a squadron of British ships.

August 16   Americans in Fort Detroit surrender.

August 19   *Constitution* defeats the British ship *Guerriere*.

September 10   Perry defeats the British on Lake Erie.

October 5   Harrison defeats British and Indian forces on the Thames River in Canada.

1814
March 27   Andrew Jackson defeats Creek Indians at Horseshoe Bend in Alabama.

August 24   British seize and burn Washington, D.C.

September 13   British bombard Fort McHenry near Baltimore.

December 24   Americans and British sign Treaty of Ghent in Belgium.

1815
January 8   Andrew Jackson leads Americans to victory over the British in New Orleans.

February 17   President James Madison declares the War of 1812 to be officially over.

Some of the most important battles in the War of 1812 took place on the water.

INTRODUCTION

A War That Served No Purpose

President Harry S Truman called the War of 1812 "the silliest damn war we ever had." Many historians agree, using such words as "unnecessary," "impractical," and "pointless" to describe the second military conflict between the United States and Great Britain. Unlike many other U.S. wars, the War of 1812 was not declared in response to an armed attack or other confrontation. There was no Pearl Harbor or sinking of the *Maine* to inflame national passions and justify sending troops into battle. Instead, the War of 1812 was the result of a steady buildup of tensions between the two countries. Over the course of many years, the two nations squabbled about British mistreatment of American sailors, British friendship with Native American Indians, as well as trade policy and taxes. With a sincere effort from both sides, most of these problems might have been resolved through peaceful means.

Before it was even begun, the War of 1812 was impractical because of the huge territories and great distances involved. The British were used to fighting within the compact, connected, and familiar lands of Europe. A war with the United States required maintaining supply lines across the vast Atlantic Ocean. It also meant marching armies through unfamiliar wilderness more than twice the size of Europe. Transportation and communication in the early 1800s were also next to impossible under these conditions. Travel by foot, horse, and ship was slow and tedious. Armies took weeks, sometimes even months, to move from one strategic point to another. Commanders on both sides of the conflict were out of touch with their superiors for long periods of

The many battles fought in the War of 1812 really did not resolve the issues that had led to the war.

time. This made it extremely difficult to effectively coordinate military operations. And it took so long for news to cross the ocean that important documents that might have prevented much of the fighting did not reach their destination in time.

The conclusion of the war underlines its pointlessness. Each side won its share of victories, but neither nation decisively defeated the other. The conflict was also a political stalemate. When a peace treaty was signed at the end of the war, none of the problems that had brought the United States and Britain to war were addressed. The peace treaty served merely to officially end the hostilities. To modern observers, the War of 1812 seems to have served no purpose.

CHAPTER ONE

The War Hawks Win the Day

I n 1800, the English-speaking peoples on both sides of the Atlantic Ocean looked forward to the new century with optimism. The British hoped that their already formidable empire would expand and bring them even more wealth and power. The many British colonies around the globe were part of an impressive trade network that made Great Britain the economic giant of its day. With a population of sixteen million, Britain maintained a huge standing army, often numbering more than 100,000 men. In addition, Britain had the world's largest, most advanced navy, making it one of the most powerful nations on earth.

The new century also seemed promising for the citizens of the infant United States. With a population of only five million, a standing army of barely four thousand men, and a tiny navy, the new nation was not an important military power. But the country controlled huge and diverse territories filled with untapped natural resources. The United States had many fine harbors on the Atlantic coastline, millions of acres of rich farmland, as well as vast forests and plains on the western and southern frontiers. This natural wealth was increased in 1803. On May 2, President Thomas Jefferson bought the Louisiana Territory from France for just fifteen million dollars. Encompassing an area of more than 800,000 square miles, the new territory almost doubled the size of the United States. The country's potential for future development and expansion now seemed nearly limitless.

The United States in 1812

When the Americans and British began fighting in 1812, the United States was already a large country. There were eighteen states—the original thirteen and five that entered the Union after 1790. These new states were Vermont (1791), Kentucky (1792), Tennessee (1796), Ohio (1803), and Louisiana, which joined the Union less than two months before the United States declared war in June 1812.

In addition to the states, the country claimed ownership of several large territories, which included, for example, what are now the states of Mississippi and Alabama. The largest U.S. territory at the time was Missouri, encompassing most of the lands of the vast Louisiana Purchase. These rolling plains and hills would later become the states of Arkansas, Missouri, Iowa, Nebraska, Kansas, and South Dakota, as well as parts of Texas, Oklahoma, Colorado, and Wyoming. In 1812, the territories were sparsely settled by both Indians and whites.

Including the states and territories, the United States stretched from New Hampshire in the north to the coast of the Gulf of Mexico in the south and from the Atlantic Ocean to the Great Plains. This huge expanse covered more than 1,680,000 square miles, an area about seventeen times larger than Great Britain. In 1812, most of the country's forests, fertile valleys, and river systems were still largely unexplored and undeveloped. Their natural riches would eventually help make the country wealthy and prosperous.

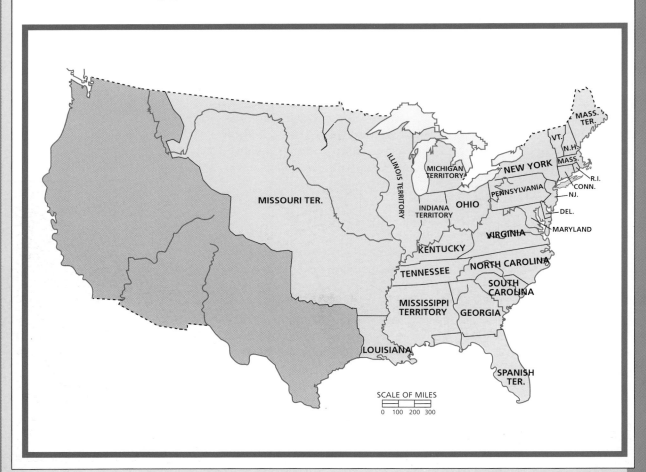

Old Problems Still Unresolved

But while both the British and Americans faced the challenges and opportunities of the new century, tensions from the old century lingered. Many in the United States remembered their fight for independence and still resented and disliked the British. Americans believed that the British social and political system was corrupt, controlled by self-serving nobles who cared little for the common people. To Americans, the British kings and queens seemed to be tyrants who were part of an outdated form of government, one inferior to the new American system of democracy.

By contrast, most British citizens were still angry and unhappy about losing the American colonies. The British looked upon Americans as undisciplined and uncultured upstarts. American democracy was viewed as a form of "mob rule," which, the British believed, would eventually collapse into chaos. Many in Britain believed that, sooner or later, the former colonies would once again come under British domination.

Old problems between the two nations seemed to get worse rather than better. During and following the American Revolution, there had been border disputes between the United States and British-controlled Canada. A boundary settlement in 1783 did not specify the exact border, and each side claimed some of the same pieces of land. The British sought to hold onto many of their forts and outposts along the Great Lakes, around which most Canadians lived. The British also tried to claim territory in

King George III of England. Americans viewed the British monarchies as outdated and corrupt.

Newly free from Britain, Americans pull down the statue of George III at the bowling green in New York City. Americans believed their system of government was a great improvement over the British monarchy.

The British surrender to General Washington. After the American Revolution, bitterness and misunderstanding continued between the British and Americans.

the Ohio Valley, Kentucky, and other sections of the frontier. This allowed them to retain control of the valuable fur trade as well as of the local Indians, who were their military allies.

To strengthen their position, the British tried to discourage American settlers from entering these areas. To accomplish this, British military commanders encouraged many of the Indian tribes to harass and attack the settlers. The attacks caused many Americans to hate and distrust nearly all Indians. Since the Americans knew who inspired the attacks, these incidents also sparked hatred and resentment of the British. Undeterred by the Indian attacks, however, American settlers continued to pour into the frontier. Between 1783 and 1812, the population of Kentucky increased from 12,000 to 400,000, and by 1810, more than 230,000 Americans had settled in the Ohio Valley. The British continued to call for Indian attacks against the settlers, and tensions steadily increased.

Disputes over Shipping

There was resentment among the British, too. After the Revolution, the two countries became trade rivals. Since Britain wanted to maintain its mastery of world sea trade, it passed laws designed to keep American ships from trading with British colonies and allies around the world. But during the 1780s and

1790s, Americans found ways to avoid these laws. Many American merchants docked and traded at small towns that were not regularly visited and policed by the British navy. Others traded with nations that were close neighbors of British colonies. These "neutral" parties shuffled goods back and forth between U.S. ships and British markets. These manipulations angered many British, especially in the wealthy classes, who saw American competition as a threat to the British economy.

To complicate matters, in 1793, Britain went to war against its longtime rival, France. The British blockaded French ports, destroyed French ships, and vowed to seize any foreign ships trying to trade with the French. This placed the United States in a

The British tried to get North American Indians to fight on the side of the British against the Americans.

A British soldier trades a gun to an Indian in exchange for American scalps. In fact, the British did encourage the Indians to attack American settlers.

Continued conflict between Great Britain and the United States resulted in a call for U.S. troops to defend against British land and sea attacks.

difficult position. Trade with France and its many colonies was important to the American economy. Americans were angry that the British had tried to keep the United States out of British markets and now tried to exclude it from French markets as well. Seeing no other choice, the Americans violated the British decree and carried on a booming trade with the French.

In retaliation, the British confiscated more than 250 American ships, an act that outraged the American public. The British also boarded many U.S. vessels at will to search for deserted British sailors. Oftentimes, they impressed, or forced, American sailors into serving in the British navy instead. This practice began because thousands of British sailors had been deserting their own ships to take jobs on American vessels due to the terrible living conditions on British ships. Because British officers were always in need of sailors to man the large number of British ships, they would often take U.S. seamen at the same time that they seized deserters.

Many angry U.S. officials demanded war with Britain over the shipping disputes and the impressment issue. But President George Washington realized that the United States was unprepared for a full-scale war and tried to avoid a conflict. He sent Chief Justice John Jay to negotiate with the British in 1794. The British knew their superior military strength gave them the advantage in the talks, and they forced Jay to accept a settlement that heavily favored the British. The settlement said the British would no longer confiscate American ships, but the Americans could no longer trade with the French and were still excluded from most British markets. Angry American mobs called the treaty a "sellout" to the British. They called Jay a traitor and burned straw dummies marked with his name. In fact, the treaty accomplished little. In the following years, British ships continued to harass American vessels, and relations between the two countries remained strained.

Maritime Troubles Intensify

As the nineteenth century dawned, renewed conflict between Britain and France once more caused problems for the United States. After nearly a decade of fighting, the British and French signed a peace treaty in 1802. But only a year later, hostilities erupted again between the two countries. In 1804, Napoleon Bonaparte, military dictator of France, prepared for a large-scale invasion of Britain, and French ships challenged Britain's control of the seas. Each side claimed the right to seize any foreign ships daring to deal with its enemy. The United States, by now the world's largest neutral trading nation, was once more caught in a dilemma. No matter which side it traded with, it would risk losing ships and sailors.

The situation worsened in 1807 when the British enacted the Orders in Council. These were rules that forbade any neutral nation from trading with any European nation except through British ports and with British licenses. The rules were designed to do two things. First, the British wanted to cut off the flow of goods into French-controlled Europe. Second, forcing U.S. and other foreign merchants to trade strictly through British ports would greatly help Britain's economy. Americans were outraged. Many American ships refused to get licenses and evaded British and French blockades. Some sneaked through under the cover of darkness. Others resorted to bribery and outright smuggling.

The British continued to seize U.S. ships and impress American sailors. The Royal Navy required at least 150,000 seamen in order to keep operating. War losses were heavy, and many British sailors, fed up with poor conditions on their own ships, continued to desert to American vessels. The British tried to fill the vacancies by forcing captured Americans into British service. Many British admirals justified these actions by refusing to recognize the independence of the United States. When seizing American sailors, they coldly proclaimed, "Once an Englishman, always an Englishman."

The most notorious seizure incident occurred in June 1807. Only ten minutes after sailing from Norfolk, Virginia, the U.S. warship *Chesapeake* encountered the British warship *Leopard*. The British captain demanded the right to examine the *Chesapeake's*

Pres. George Washington sent Chief Justice John Jay (below) to negotiate with the British over shipping disputes and impressment.

Thomas Jefferson, third president of the United States, is recognized as one of its greatest leaders.

crew. He had reason to believe that a British deserter named Jenkin Ratford, who had publicly denounced the British, was aboard. The captain of the American ship, James Barron, was furious. This was the first time that the British had tried to take seamen from a naval vessel. All former incidents involved merchant ships. Barron angrily refused the British demand. The *Leopard* then blasted the *Chesapeake* with its cannon. Unprepared for combat, the *Chesapeake* suffered heavy damage, and Barron had to give in. Several British officers boarded the crippled ship and seized Ratford. They also impressed three American sailors.

Some members of Congress, outraged by the *Chesapeake* incident, demanded immediate war with Britain. But these war hawks, as they were called, were not in the majority. Most U.S. lawmakers backed President Jefferson, who had what he thought was a better alternative to war. Jefferson decided to teach both the British and the French a lesson. He cut off trade with the two countries and also with the countries that traded with them. This, he reasoned, would hurt the countries economically and force them to come to terms with the Americans. In December 1807, Congress passed Jefferson's Embargo Act, which kept American ships bound for any foreign nation from leaving U.S. ports.

But the embargo was a failure. Rather than being hurt by the move, the British profited by taking over the share of foreign trade that the Americans had given up. At the same time, the overall loss of trade for the United States severely damaged the American economy. The British maintained the Orders in Council and continued impressing American seamen. Just before leaving office in 1809, Jefferson lifted the U.S. embargo. But the damage had been done. The American economy continued to suffer, and the United States appeared weak and powerless in the eyes of the European powers.

Economic Troubles

Although most of the United States suffered financially from the effects of the embargo, a few parts of the country actually profited. Some U.S. merchants, particularly those living in the New England states where smuggling was already widespread, ignored the rules and became rich by conducting illegal, secret trade with foreign nations. They also made special deals with the British and continued to receive British goods and money. The British made these deals hoping to get New England to break away from the United States and ally itself with Britain. This illegal trade made the embargo largely ineffective.

Few New Englanders wanted war with Britain. They were furious over the embargo and opposed U.S. policies so strongly that they often claimed to feel more British than American. Congressmen from New England argued that a war with Britain

Thomas Jefferson—Patriot and Pacifist

As the third U.S. president, Thomas Jefferson is recognized as one of the country's greatest leaders. He was born in the British colony of Virginia in 1743 and graduated from William and Mary College in 1762. After practicing law for a time, he entered politics and began sharply criticizing British rule. He kept in constant touch with patriots in other colonies and became influential as a leader of the American independence movement. Because of Jefferson's political skill and eloquent writing style, the other founders asked him to draft the Declaration of Independence. Later, he served as ambassador to France as well as secretary of state under George Washington and vice president under John Adams.

Jefferson became president on March 4, 1801. He believed that the president was a servant of the people and should not use a lot of ceremony to distance himself from those he governed or from Congress. In order to make the office of president easily approachable to the Congress, Jefferson eliminated many of the formal customs practiced during the administrations of Washington and Adams. For example, both former presidents had made periodic visits to Congress. On these occasions, they had delivered long, formal speeches in order to introduce new ideas or suggest new laws. Jefferson replaced these lofty and time-consuming speeches with simple written messages expressing his views.

Jefferson also eliminated other ceremonies. Washington and Adams had both met with foreign diplomats or members of Congress according to formal rules. Whoever had the highest rank saw the president first. And few met him at dinner, which was considered too informal and personal an occasion for conducting affairs of state. Jefferson introduced the custom of large state dinners, where guests took whatever seat was available, regardless of rank, and all approached the president on an equal basis. Jefferson also gave many smaller dinners. Some of these he served himself, wearing slippers and other informal attire.

Although he had recognized the necessity of fighting Britain during the Revolution, Jefferson was at heart a pacifist. His dream was to see the United States develop peacefully, unspoiled by the rivalries and hatreds that continued to wrack Europe. Therefore, he was strongly against getting involved in the Napoleonic Wars of the early 1800s. But trade with both the British and French was essential to the U.S. economy, and sooner or later, the Americans would have to deal with one side and risk war with the other. Jefferson's Embargo Act of 1807 was an earnest but unsuccessful attempt to force both the British and French to deal fairly with his country.

Jefferson's most memorable and lasting achievement as president was acquiring the Louisiana Purchase from France in 1803. This land instantly doubled the size of the United States and gave the country great future potential for wealth and expansion. He also sent explorers Meriwether Lewis and William Clark to investigate the western frontier, where they discovered the natural wonders and riches that lay far beyond the Mississippi River.

After two terms as president, Jefferson retired to his Virginia home, Monticello. There, he pursued his many interests, including the study of music, science, literature, and foreign languages. He could read and write Latin, Greek, French, Spanish, and Italian, among others. A brilliant architect, he designed the University of Virginia, overseeing every detail of its construction. He ardently studied fossils unearthed in New York and sincerely attempted to trace the ancestry of American Indians and blacks. Perhaps the most talented and versatile statesman the United States has ever known, Jefferson died on July 4, 1826. Many called the date appropriate. It was exactly fifty years to the day after the Declaration of Independence was proclaimed and the United States was born.

James Madison succeeded Thomas Jefferson as president. When economic troubles continued to plague the United States, Madison reinstated a trade embargo against the British.

would totally ruin the U.S. economy. They insisted that the United States and Britain settle their differences peacefully. Many threatened to secede from, or leave, the Union rather than fight.

But people in other parts of the country were not convinced that Britain would listen and respond to American grievances. The American embargo had been lifted, but the British Orders in Council restricting U.S. shipping remained. The continued loss of trade brought economic troubles to the American South, the area stretching from Virginia southward to Georgia and the Mississippi Territory. Farmers found fewer and fewer markets for their crops and many Americans lost their jobs. The West, including Ohio, Tennessee, and Kentucky, also suffered. With no one to buy their grain, thousands of western farmers had huge surpluses and faced financial ruin. In 1810, large sections of the South and West suffered an economic depression. Public support for the war hawks, who came mainly from these areas, grew steadily.

Economic troubles in the United States became even worse after President James Madison succeeded Jefferson as president. The French tricked Madison into reinstating the embargo against Britain late in 1810. Napoleon wanted to keep as much economic pressure on Britain as possible. So he led Madison to believe that the French would lift their own restrictions against U.S. shipping if the Americans resumed the embargo against Britain. Madison put the embargo back into effect, but the French did not keep their part of the bargain. Napoleon's only intention had been to hurt the British and he had succeeded. Napoleon reasoned that he could get away with not honoring the deal with the United States because the Americans had no practical way to retaliate against him. Despite this treachery, Madison maintained the embargo against the British. He stubbornly continued to hope that the embargo would eventually hurt the British economy enough to force suspension of the Orders in Council.

Problems on the Frontier

While the Americans continued to endure British shipping restrictions and confrontations at sea, American-British disputes along the frontier began to heat up. The British increased their efforts to arm the Indians and incite them against American settlers. In 1810, the Indian attacks escalated into full-scale war between whites and pro-British tribes such as the Shawnee and Potawatomi.

The most important Indian leader was the great Shawnee chief Tecumseh. He had good reason to ally himself with the British against the Americans. As a young man, he had seen his father and elder brothers killed while resisting white settlers who seized Shawnee land. In the early 1800s, Tecumseh tried to unite the tribes of the northwestern frontier into a single, strong alliance. An intelligent and skilled leader, he preached that the Indians must stand together against the increasing flood of white settlers. He foresaw that the whites would eventually take over all Indian lands and subdue the tribes. Hoping to retain control of the Indian hunting grounds of the Great Lakes region, Tecumseh began attacking American settlements in the Indiana Territory.

In November 1811, William Henry Harrison, recently appointed governor of the Indiana Territory, attacked Tecumseh's forces. Leading a force of some nine hundred troops, Harrison camped near Tippecanoe Creek in northern Indiana. Across the creek stood the large village commanded by Tecumseh's brother, known as the Prophet. Loudmouthed and with few leadership abilities, the Prophet claimed to be able to see into the future. On the evening of November 6, he chanted before a huge bonfire, then told his followers that he had cast a spell over the American camp. Half of the whites were now dead, he claimed, and the other half were driven insane. It would be an easy matter to attack and finish them off. The Prophet added that the white leader, who rode a gray horse, must be killed as quickly as possible.

Early on the cold, rainy morning of November 7, more than two thousand Indians gathered in the woods near Harrison's camp. After an American sentry spotted them and opened fire, the Prophet's warriors attacked. Awakened by the sound of musket fire, Harrison ran from his tent and jumped onto his aide's horse by mistake. The aide took Harrison's horse and died a few minutes later when the Indians mistook him for Harrison. Screaming loudly, the Indians launched three furious attacks. Normally, they would have moved forward slowly, taking advantage of the cover of rocks and trees. But the Prophet's vision had foretold that the whites were nearly defenseless. So, the Indians approached in the open, running headlong at the American lines. Harrison's men drove them back each time, inflicting heavy losses on the Prophet's warriors. Soon, the Indians discovered that the Prophet had deserted them. Then, the warriors also panicked and fled. Later that day, Harrison ordered the Prophet's village burned to the ground.

Tecumseh (top) attempted to unite all North American Indian tribes into one fighting force against the United States. His brother, Prophet,(bottom) foolishly ignored Tecumseh's advice to avoid attacking the whites without reinforcements. As a result, Prophet's village was destroyed.

Harrison's victory at Tippecanoe significantly increased tensions between the United States and the British-Indian alliance. Tecumseh, enraged by his brother's defeat, firmly sided with the British, who supplied the Indians with more arms than ever and urged them to continue their attacks on the settlers. This further outraged Americans, especially the war hawks in Congress. They bitterly recalled that the British and Indians had formed a deadly alliance during the Revolution. They warned that the same thing seemed to be happening again.

The hawks not only demanded war but wanted the United

An artist's depiction of the Battle of Tippecanoe. Acting on the advice of Prophet, the Indians rushed headlong into the American lines.

States to invade Canada. This would remove British influence from the northwestern frontier once and for all. The hawks interpreted Harrison's win at Tippecanoe as proof that the Americans could easily defeat British and Indian forces. Despite the confidence of the war hawks, the American forces were not prepared to fight an extended war. The U.S. Army numbered only about seven thousand in 1811, and most units were ill trained and scattered over the entire country. Nevertheless, the hawks continued to press for an attack on Canada.

Though they did not admit it openly, the hawks saw taking Canada as only the first step toward a larger goal. They believed, along with many other Americans, that as the population of the United States grew, new territories would be needed to accommodate these people. To some, it seemed inevitable that Americans would eventually control all of North America. After taking over Canada, the United States would secure the Indian lands of Illinois, Tennessee, and far beyond, territories rich in fertile land, fresh water, and animal furs. Eventually, the hawks proposed, the United States would control Florida and other lands owned by the Spanish. The main obstacle to achieving this goal at the moment was Britain, which wanted to retain an area of control

Henry Clay—The Great Compromiser

Henry Clay (1777-1852) was one of the most influential and powerful U.S. politicians of the first half of the nineteenth century. Born in Virginia, he became a lawyer and moved to Kentucky. By 1800, Clay was recognized as one of Kentucky's finest lawyers. Because of his strong opinions and flair for oratory, he became involved in politics and was elected to the Kentucky legislature in 1803. Although he strongly supported Jefferson's policies, he showed that he was willing to give in sometimes to the views of his opponents in order to get a bill passed. This earned him a reputation as an effective compromiser.

Clay became a U.S. senator in 1809 and a member of the House of Representatives in 1811. There, he led a group of ardent expansionists popularly known as the war hawks. Clay and his colleagues demanded that the United States declare war on Britain over such issues as British impressment of American sailors and unfair restrictions on U.S. shipping. On November 11, 1811, Clay was elected Speaker of the House. Before this time, the Speaker had exerted little control over House members, who often interrupted each other and spoke out of turn. Clay enforced stricter rules of order and made the Speaker a more powerful figure.

In the years following the War of 1812, Clay continued to play an important role in U.S. politics. In 1820, when the South and the North were battling over which states should be designated slave states and which free states, he successfully negotiated a compromise that held for several years. For his efforts in this respect, Clay became known as "the great compromiser."

As the Speaker of the House of Representatives, Henry Clay led the war hawk faction, a group that wanted to go to war with Britain.

and influence in North America. War with and victory over Britain, reasoned the hawks, would clear the way for American expansion.

The Nation Drifts Toward War

No single event brought the two countries to the brink of war. Instead, the maritime and economic disputes and the frontier troubles of nearly three decades continued to pile up. Many Americans felt helpless and wanted the country to take a firm stand, even if it meant war. But the antiwar groups continued to control the Congress.

But a declaration of war became possible with the elections of 1811. Voters in the West and South were sick of the economic troubles and Indian attacks caused by the British. They elected to Congress about forty influential western and southern war hawks, who made the pro-war faction a majority for the first time. This group was led by Kentucky's forceful and energetic Henry Clay, who was elected Speaker of the House of Representatives. This gave him the power to appoint hawks as heads of important committees, including those controlling foreign relations, military affairs, and the navy. Now, every British insult, no matter how small, was enthusiastically denounced in Congress. The hawks convinced Madison to demand that the British remove their Orders in Council restricting American shipping. Madison did so, sending a written demand by ship to Britain. But there was no response from the British, and by May 1812, many American leaders decided it was finally time to fight.

What the Americans did not know was that Madison's embargo had been working. By the early months of 1812, the British had begun to feel the economic effects of the embargo. Many British politicians argued that the country needed American trade and called for suspending the Orders in Council. But members of Prime Minister Spencer Perceval's government wanted to keep the Orders. On May 11, 1812, a madman shot Perceval, bringing the government to a standstill. Now lacking Perceval's support, his followers agreed to suspend the Orders in Council on June 16. Because news of these events had to travel on slow ships over a great distance, the report of the suspension did not reach the United States until it was too late. On June 18, just two days after the major obstacle to peace had been removed, the United States declared war on Great Britain. The war hawks had won the day at last. But many worried Americans wondered if they could win the war.

CHAPTER TWO

The Disastrous Canadian Campaign

I n the summer of 1812, the United States was officially at war with one of the world's great powers. The president, members of Congress, and military leaders all agreed that the best chance for the United States was to defeat the British on land. The British navy was far more powerful than the tiny U.S. fleet, and the Americans were convinced that there was no chance of a victory at sea. U.S. leaders unanimously decided to attack and capture the British-Canadian forts and towns in the Great Lakes region, which was where British power in North America was concentrated. Taking Canada would not only remove the British from the continent but also expand the size of the United States.

At first, Americans were confident and enthusiastic about their ability to defeat the British. To American leaders and citizens, it seemed that an attack on Canada could not fail. One factor in the Americans' favor was that the population of Canada was only about 500,000, whereas the population of the United States was nearly 7,500,000. Although the U.S. Army was very small, the country's large population meant it had the potential to raise more troops than the Canadians. Another U.S. advantage was that the British had to defend a border some seventeen hundred miles long with fewer than eight thousand troops. There would be few reinforcements because most of Britain's huge army was occupied with fighting Napoleon in Europe. Although the British had thousands of Indian allies, American military officers were sure that their army could readily defeat the Indians, whom most Americans regarded as undisciplined savages. Harrison's easy victory at Tippecanoe seemed proof of American superiority over the Indians.

Generals Henry Dearborn (top) and William Hull were unfit to lead armies during the War of 1812.

But, in fact, the United States was not prepared for this war. The military had so many problems that its conquest of Canada was doomed from the start. The seven thousand soldiers in the regular army had little training, and most had no battle experience. There were also about fifty thousand militiamen, farmers, and businessmen who could be called up to fight during an emergency. But the militia was under the command of individual state governors, who refused to enter the national fight unless the states themselves were directly attacked. So, the federal government had to make do with the tiny regular army for its Canadian campaign.

The men in the U.S. Army suffered serious morale problems. Many of the soldiers did not want a military career and had signed up for only a year or so to see what being in the army was like. Often, they decided they hated military life and then talked about little else but going home. During the late 1700s and early 1800s, it became common for soldiers to pack up and leave when their term of enlistment was over, even on the eve of an important battle. Supply problems also contributed to poor morale. Transporting tons of supplies to distant armies across hundreds of thousands of square miles of untamed wilderness was difficult and sometimes impossible. In addition, there often was not enough money in the U.S. Treasury to pay for the huge amounts of supplies needed, which meant the troops were forced to do without adequate food and clothing.

A Sad Lack of Leadership and Planning

Adding to the army's manpower and morale problems was its lack of strong leadership. Nearly all the American generals were too old and incompetent to command troops in wartime. Many had seen brief service in the Revolution thirty years before but knew little about strategy or commanding troops. They had received their present military titles through political connections. The senior major general, Henry Dearborn, was sixty-one and had fought at Bunker Hill in the 1770s. He was so feeble and out of touch with military life that his men called him Granny. At sixty, Brig. Gen. William Hull, governor of the Michigan Territory, was also unfit to lead an army. He had no leadership abilities and had never planned a military campaign. A friend described him as "a short, corpulent [fat], good-natured old gentleman who bore the marks of good eating and drinking."

The American army had still another major shortcoming. American leaders had taken the country into war with no overall strategy in mind. Everyone knew that the major goal was to conquer Canada, but no one had suggested how this formidable task should be accomplished. It was William Hull who finally came up with a plan. In a meeting with President Madison and his aides,

James Madison

James Madison was the fourth president of the United States. He was born in Virginia in 1751 and attended Princeton University. He was the youngest of the Founding Fathers attending the Continental Congress in 1780 during the American Revolution. Later, in 1787, he was a key member of the group that framed the U.S. Constitution at the Constitutional Convention. Madison himself drafted the Bill of Rights and kept careful notes of the proceedings. Much of what is known about the convention comes from these notes. In 1794, Madison married a young widow named Dolley Payne Todd. She would later become one of the nation's most popular first ladies. Cultured, charming, and hardworking, she frequently entertained guests at the White House, making their visits enjoyable and memorable.

During Thomas Jefferson's presidency, Madison served as secretary of state and worked closely with the president. Madison himself ran for president in 1808. Leaders of the New England states strongly opposed him because he had earlier backed Jefferson's Embargo Act against the British and French. This law was already having a negative effect on the economy of New England as well as on some other parts of the nation. But thanks to Jefferson's support and votes from the western and southern states, Madison easily won the election.

In 1812, the war hawks in Congress pushed Madison to declare war on Great Britain. New Englanders and others who opposed the war called the conflict "Mr. Madison's war." They quickly blamed Madison for the long series of American defeats in Canada. After the British invaded and burned Washington in 1814, Madison lost much support and respect. With the Treasury empty because of the trade embargo and the war effort, there was a real chance that the government might fall apart. But the subsequent Treaty of Ghent and American victory in New Orleans restored Madison's popularity.

Pres. James Madison led the country during the War of 1812. Much as presidents today, he was heavily criticized when the United States appeared to be losing the war.

Madison retired from office in 1817, leaving the country more united and with a brighter future than when he first became president. He died in 1836, outliving all the other Founding Fathers.

Hull proposed that an army be sent to American-held Fort Detroit, located in a strategic position on the western shore of Lake Erie. The British, claimed Hull, would be intimidated by this show of force and would quickly abandon that section of Canada. Someone pointed out that the British had warships patrolling the lakes, and that the United States might also need to build a fleet for the lakes. But Hull insisted that this would not be necessary. He assured Madison that the British, during their retreat, would abandon their fleet and leave the ships in American hands.

Madison not only went along with Hull's fantastic, poorly conceived plan but also approved plans suggested by General Dearborn. Dearborn's idea was to launch an attack along the length of Lake Champlain in northern New York State and strike at the Canadian city of Montreal, about fifty miles farther north. At the same time, armies from Detroit, Fort Niagara, and other points near the Great Lakes would move northward into the Montreal region. The American leaders believed that all of Canada would fall in the space of a few months. With Madison's blessing, Hull immediately took charge of a force of two thousand men and confidently marched them through the Ohio Valley toward Detroit.

Fear and Indecision

But Hull's confidence faded quickly. The trail was difficult and treacherous. The forests were thick and filled with swamps, and many of his men caught malaria. Some, in poor physical condition, dropped dead from exhaustion. Morale declined rapidly, and the soldiers often fought among themselves. Hull seemed to lack the strength and courage needed to instill proper discipline in his troops.

Eventually, Hull and his men reached the Maumee River, which flows through northern Indiana and into Lake Erie about sixty miles south of Detroit. By chance, they found a small American ship, the *Cuyahoga,* moored along the riverbank. Hull loaded his cannons and other heavy equipment into the ship and ordered the crew to sail for Detroit. Freed of carrying and dragging this equipment, Hull reasoned that he and his men could make better time through the wilderness. But Hull made a serious blunder. He put a trunk containing his military plans and lists of men and equipment on board the ship. The *Cuyahoga* sped down the river, entered Lake Erie, and made for Detroit. But the British, whose ships controlled the lakes, captured the American ship on July 2, 1812. Unknown to Hull, the enemy had also captured his plans and knew his troop strength.

Meanwhile, the British tried to prepare for an American invasion. Gen. George Prevost, commander of all the Canadian provinces, was worried that the British position was weak. He did not have enough men to patrol and defend the entire border, and he was unsure of where the Americans would strike first. He ordered Gen. Isaac Brock, commander of the region surrounding Lakes Erie and Ontario, not to provoke a fight.

But Brock, a brilliant soldier, filled with energy and determination, ignored his superior. Brock believed that it was important to go on the offensive and attack right away in order to keep up the morale of his British and Indian troops. He had earlier shown his excellent grasp of strategy by expanding the British lakes fleet, which was the key to control of the entire region. With their ships, the British could quickly ferry men and supplies from one Canadian fort or town to another. Brock reasoned that the Americans' strongest chance for penetrating Canada would be an attack on the Niagara region between Lakes Erie and Ontario. This could effectively disrupt British supply lines moving from one lake to another. Brock did not anticipate that the American generals would ignore their best opportunity. So, unaware that Hull was nearing Detroit, Brock rushed his forces to the Niagara River and ordered them to prepare for an assault.

Hull and his men arrived at Fort Detroit on July 5, 1812. The fort, covering two acres, housed about eight hundred people and guarded more than five thousand American farmers and other civilians in the area. Among the residents of the fort were Hull's daughter and grandchildren. Hull's men were itching for a fight and urged him to order an attack on nearby Fort Malden, located on the Canadian side of Lake Erie. There were few British troops defending Fort Malden at the time, and it would have been an easy first victory for the Americans. But Hull was indecisive. He changed his mind constantly, first ordering an attack, then canceling the order. As the days dragged on, he appeared to become more and more nervous and afraid. He discovered that the *Cuyahoga* had been captured, along with his trunk of information, and feared a British attack at any moment. He also feared that Fort Detroit would soon run out of supplies. So, in late July, he ordered six hundred of his men to march south toward Ohio and bring back as many supplies as possible.

Surrender and Dishonor

But Hull's supply detail did not get far. The unfortunate group encountered Tecumseh and his Indians near the Raisin River, about fifty miles south of Detroit. With only seventy warriors and forty British regulars, Tecumseh surprised the much larger American force. Terrified and unprepared for a fight, the Americans retreated in confusion, and Tecumseh's warriors killed the stragglers one by one. The few survivors fled at top speed back to Detroit and reported the incident to the horrified William Hull.

Tecumseh (astride horse) proved to be a remarkably good leader of men. He was able to win battles against superior numbers and weapons through organization, leadership, and will.

At the same time, General Brock arrived at Fort Detroit, having heard about Hull's mission several days earlier. Brock loaded his men onto a ship and sped across Lake Erie to Detroit, proving the strategic value of controlling the lakes. Brock met with Tecumseh, congratulated him on his victory, and made him an honorary brigadier general. Together, the two skilled leaders examined the information from Hull's trunk and planned how to take Detroit. Brock admitted that he had no reliable maps of the area. Without hesitation, Tecumseh took out his scalping knife and carved an amazingly accurate map on a piece of birch bark.

In the meantime, Hull seemed on the verge of a nervous breakdown. He had visions of his grandchildren's scalps, as well as his own, hanging in Tecumseh's lodge. Hull feared that the Indians would attack not only Detroit but also other forts and towns in the region. Because he was now the ranking officer in the area, the safety of these settlements, including Fort Dearborn, about 250 miles west of Detroit, was his responsibility. He was sure there would be massacres for which his superiors would blame him. He sent a message to Capt. William Wells, who commanded a small American garrison about 100 miles away in Indiana. Hull ordered Wells to rush to Fort Dearborn and evacuate all soldiers and civilians before any hostile Indians arrived.

Wells reached Fort Dearborn on August 12, 1812, and found the area already swarming with Indians led by Tecumseh's ally, the Potawatomi chief Blackbird. Wells attempted to lead the settlers and troops out of the fort three days later. But Blackbird and five hundred of his warriors caught and surrounded them only an hour after they left the fort.

Wells, who had lived for some years among the Indians, realized that there was no escape, that none of the Americans would get out alive. Deciding to die fighting, he moistened his hands and spread black gunpowder over his face, an Indian sign of defiance. He then bravely galloped his horse directly at Blackbird. Wells called the Indians "miserable squaws" and screamed every Indian insult he knew. Blackbird himself shot Wells, killing him instantly. The chief then enacted an old tribal custom that paid tribute to a brave enemy. The Indians believed that courage dwelled within the heart and that a warrior could absorb his enemy's courage. The Americans watched in horror as Blackbird slit open Wells's chest, removed the heart, and ate it raw. The Indians then massacred the rest of Wells's party.

While Wells and his men battled Blackbird, many miles to the east Brock and Tecumseh closed in on Fort Detroit and the terrified William Hull. Brock ordered British warships on Lake Erie to spray the fort with cannon fire while Tecumseh's warriors surrounded the enclosure. Hull's men wanted to fight, but he was too frightened and upset to organize an offensive. At daybreak on August 16, 1812, the Americans in the fort watched in disgust as Hull fell apart before their eyes. He sat against the wall, his voice trembling, his eyes flitting from side to side. He stuffed one wad of chewing tobacco after another into his mouth until the brown

The stress of battle was too much for elderly Gen. William Hull, even though he had more soldiers than the attacking British. American soldiers under his command were shocked and dismayed when he ordered them to surrender to the British.

The Reliable and Deadly Musket

The musket, or flintlock, was a primitive rifle used extensively by the world's armies from the 1500s to the 1800s. The weapon helped make the Spanish, who invented it, a world power in the 1500s. One loaded a musket by pouring gunpowder down the front barrel, then inserting a lead ball. When the trigger was pulled, a metal hammer struck a piece of flint. This produced a spark, which ignited the powder. The explosion pushed the ball out of the barrel. Muskets could fire up to two hundred yards, but it took almost a minute to load one and they were not very accurate. Nevertheless, except for cannons, they were the most reliable and deadly weapons available.

A major advance in musket design occurred in 1801. The U.S. government hired Eli Whitney, the inventor of the cotton gin, to produce thousands of muskets for the American army. This was a tremendously difficult and expensive task at the time. For centuries, people had made the weapons and their individual parts by hand, and no two muskets were exactly alike. It normally took one person an entire week to make just one musket. Whitney realized he had to create machines and other labor-saving devices in order to successfully mass-produce the rifles.

With a government advance of only five thousand dollars, Whitney set up a musket-making factory in New Haven, Connecticut. The design of the plant became a model for most other American industrial plants of the nineteenth century. Whitney had the novel idea of making muskets with interchangeable parts. He invented special machine tools that quickly turned out identical parts that easily fit together, making each weapon the same.

Whitney invited a group of congressmen and cabinet members, including Thomas Jefferson, to gather around a table. The table was covered with dozens of assorted musket pieces. He challenged them to put the pieces together, then load and fire the weapon. They completed the task and were so impressed that they gave Whitney three times the money he had asked for to further develop the idea.

The musket was used by armies for over three centuries. In 1801, Eli Whitney made the musket even more easy to use for large numbers of troops when he invented interchangeable parts for the weapon.

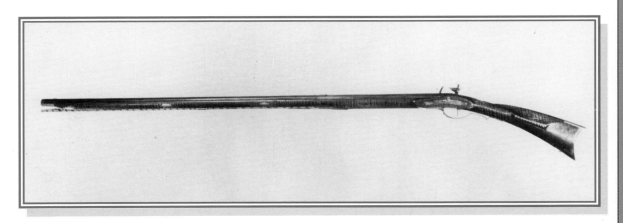

Many Indian tribes joined Tecumseh's fight against the whites, including the Sac tribe, pictured here readying for war.

spittle dribbled out and ran down his chest. A few minutes later, he sent word to General Brock that the fort would surrender.

Hull's men, enraged by the disgrace, threw down their weapons. Some wept openly as the British marched into the fort. One of the Americans later wrote to his brother, "We could have whipped hell out of the rascals but General Hull has proved himself a traitor and a coward.... We were made to submit to the most shameful surrender that ever took place in the world. Our brave Captain Harry James cursed and swore like a pirate, and cried like his heart would break." It was the first and only surrender of an American city to a foreign foe. So ended William Hull's master plan for the conquest of Canada.

Defeat and Failure

News of the fall of Detroit swiftly spread across the country. Emboldened by the victory, many Indian tribes that had earlier refused to join Tecumseh's federation now flocked to his side. The Sac, Winnebago, and Ottawa tribes came, as did bands of Cherokee, Creek, Delaware, and Kickapoo. The Great Lakes frontier exploded with ambushes and massacres of American settlers. Terrified and defenseless, thousands of white homesteaders fled eastward. The British moved south into American territory and built a fort on the Raisin River. This was not only a move of strategic importance but also a slap in the face of American honor.

Meanwhile, the American public called for William Hull's head. The fall of Detroit had brought shame and dishonor upon the nation. Even Thomas Jefferson, known for his understanding

Sir Isaac Brock

Isaac Brock (1769-1812) was one of Great Britain's most gifted military officers. He entered the army in 1785 and quickly worked his way up through the ranks. He became a lieutenant colonel when only twenty-eight, an unusual feat at the time.

In 1802, the British stationed Brock in Canada. There, he had no trouble in attaining a series of important and powerful positions. In 1810, Brock was given command of the British troops in upper Canada, the area around Lakes Ontario and Erie. He expanded and improved the British fleet of ships on the lakes believing that control of the lakes was vital to the defense of Canada. He continued to earn promotions, becoming a major general in 1811.

When war broke out in the summer of 1812, Brock masterminded the successful British strategy against the Americans. He used ships to swiftly move an army across Lake Erie and capture Fort Detroit from the Americans. Later, Brock soundly defeated the U.S. Army near the Niagara River. But during this battle, he was shot and killed. Three days before his death, the British king awarded Brock a knighthood for taking Detroit. But because it took weeks for news to cross the ocean, Brock never learned of the honor.

and forgiving nature, angrily called Hull's actions "treacherous." Eventually, a military court tried Hull and sentenced him to death for cowardice in the line of duty. At the last minute, Madison spared his life. Many Americans said the president was being too generous.

Thirsting for revenge against the British and Indians, thousands of Americans in Kentucky and Tennessee enlisted in the army. They joined a force commanded by William Henry Harrison, the hero of Tippecanoe. Harrison replaced Hull as commander of all American troops in the northwestern frontier. In late September 1812, Harrison led ten thousand troops northward with the goal of retaking Detroit. But the army encountered heavy autumn rains that created deep layers of mud and swelled the rivers and swamps. The wilderness became impassable, and Harrison decided to wait for winter. Then, he reasoned, the rivers and lakes would freeze over and his men could easily reach Detroit across the ice. He encamped his army and waited.

Meanwhile, General Brock, in command of sixteen hundred British troops and three hundred Indians, hurried back to the Niagara region. He had received word that the Americans were preparing to launch an attack across the Niagara River. Brock's small force faced an American army of more than six thousand. The U.S. troops were led by Stephen Van Rensselaer, a recently appointed general who had no previous military experience. Once again, Brock's military genius, combined with incompetent American leadership, spelled disaster for the Americans. Van Rensselaer led about eight hundred U.S. soldiers across the river, believing that the rest of the army would cross downstream and join them. But for unknown reasons, most of the rest of the Americans refused to cross and the British and Indians attacked Van Rensselaer's group. Most of Van Rensselaer's eight hundred men were hacked to pieces or drowned in the turbulent river as the rest of his troops sat on the opposite bank and did nothing.

In a sense, the battle ended up being both a victory and a defeat for the British. They clearly triumphed and brought further disgrace to the Americans, but during the fighting, Isaac Brock took a shot in the chest and died. Never again would the British have a commander of his talent and stature in Canada. Brock's death greatly decreased the chances for a British victory in a prolonged land war.

Other American embarrassments and defeats soon followed. In November 1812, Gen. Alexander Smythe led a force of six thousand U.S. troops to the Niagara River with the intention of entering Canada. The soldiers boarded boats and were less than halfway across when Smythe ordered a retreat. Without offering any explanation, he simply called off the expedition. According to some witnesses, Smythe's men were so enraged that they shot

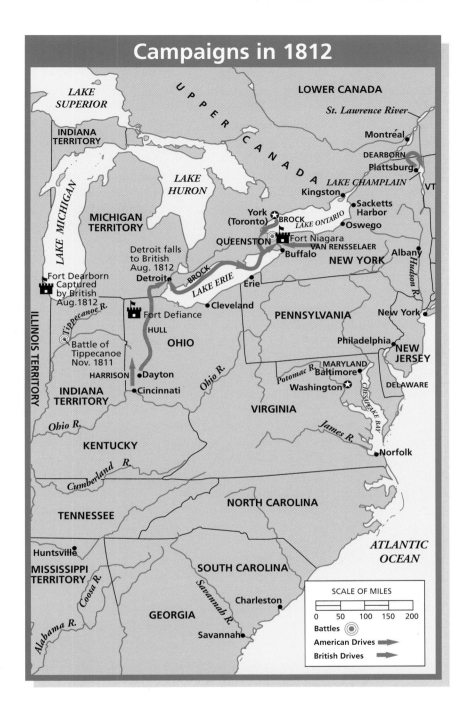

Campaigns in 1812

LAKE SUPERIOR

INDIANA TERRITORY

UPPER CANADA

LOWER CANADA

St. Lawrence River

Montréal

DEARBORN
Plattsburg

LAKE CHAMPLAIN

VT

Kingston

Sacketts Harbor

Oswego

York (Toronto)

BROCK

LAKE ONTARIO

Fort Niagara

VAN RENSSELAER

Albany

LAKE HURON

LAKE MICHIGAN

MICHIGAN TERRITORY

Detroit falls to British Aug. 1812

Detroit

BROCK

QUEENSTON

Buffalo

NEW YORK

LAKE ERIE

Erie

Hudson R.

Fort Dearborn Captured by British Aug.1812

Tippecanoe R.

Fort Defiance

HULL

Cleveland

PENNSYLVANIA

New York

ILLINOIS TERRITORY

Battle of Tippecanoe Nov. 1811

HARRISON

OHIO

Dayton

Cincinnati

Ohio R.

Philadelphia

NEW JERSEY

MARYLAND

Baltimore

DELAWARE

Potomac R.

Washington

CHESAPEAKE BAY

INDIANA TERRITORY

Ohio R.

VIRGINIA

James R.

KENTUCKY

Cumberland R.

Norfolk

TENNESSEE

NORTH CAROLINA

Huntsville

MISSISSIPPI TERRITORY

Coosa R.

SOUTH CAROLINA

Savannah R.

ATLANTIC OCEAN

Charleston

GEORGIA

Savannah

Alabama R.

SCALE OF MILES

0 50 100 150 200

Battles ◉
American Drives ➡
British Drives ➡

him, taking care to make it look like an accident. Dearborn's attempt to cross Lake Champlain and capture Montreal fared no better. His force of seven thousand men engaged about nineteen hundred British Canadians north of the lake on the evening of November 19. After only a few minutes of fighting, the British wisely retreated. Then, the Americans got lost and began firing on each other. Later, they informed Dearborn that they would go no farther, and many left because their enlistments were up. The embarrassed Dearborn had no choice but to cancel the rest of the campaign.

The plans for a grand conquest of Canada turned into a sad demonstration of the lack of military planning and leadership on the part of the United States. As historian Robert Leckie put it, the campaign was "the most inglorious chapter in American military history." By early 1813, thousands of American soldiers and settlers had died, and the frontier was more dangerous and disorganized than ever. Britain retained control of the Great Lakes and made the U.S. Army a laughingstock. Many members of Congress blamed Madison, saying that he should have appointed better, more experienced officers. They also faulted him for not building a Great Lakes fleet, which they came to regard as essential in gaining control of the region. As the president worked to correct these mistakes, he reminded his critics that all was not lost. During the same months that the land campaigns on the frontier were bogged down in mud and disgrace, American warships had heroically turned defeat into victory and were the pride of the nation.

CHAPTER THREE

Victories on the Open Sea

When the United States declared war on Great Britain in June 1812, American leaders planned to use the small U.S. fleet mainly to defend the Atlantic coast. They also hoped to capture or destroy some of the British cargo ships carrying supplies bound for Canada. Challenging British warships for mastery of the Atlantic seemed out of the question. After all, the British Royal Navy was by far the largest in the world, and no one on either side believed the United States stood a chance on the open seas.

British naval power was immense. In 1812, Britain had more than 600 warships, including 120 ships of the line. A ship of the line, carrying between fifty and eighty cannons, was an early version of a modern battleship. The British also had 116 frigates, smaller and faster than ships of the line and able to carry between thirty-two and forty-four big guns. These ships were commanded by superb officers and manned with well-trained, experienced crews. No one in the world doubted that British naval power was invincible. Although the bulk of Britain's navy was engaged in the European war, the several dozen warships committed to American waters appeared to be more than enough to deal with the tiny U.S. fleet. With complete confidence, British naval officers looked with contempt on their "inferior" American counterparts.

Outgunned but Eager to Fight

At the time, the Americans had only sixteen warships capable of operating on the open seas. They had no ships of the line and only seven frigates. The others were mere sloops, single-masted vessels capable of carrying only a few small cannons. The frigates, including the *Constitution* and *United States,* had been built in the 1790s. They were well-constructed and expertly commanded but faced the incredible task of patrolling nearly two thousand miles of U.S. coastline. The navy also had about two hundred small gunboats. But no match for large warships, these were good only for defensive purposes inside shallow harbors. Though heavily outnumbered and outgunned by the British, the American navy had one significant advantage. U.S. naval officers were young, brash, and eager to show the arrogant British captains what American sailors were made of.

Only a few hours after the American declaration of war on June 18, 1812, thirty-five-year-old Capt. Isaac Hull received his orders from Madison's war planners. He was to sail his ship, the frigate *Constitution,* from Annapolis, Maryland, to New York to defend against a possible British attack. The orders emphasized the official American naval strategy: No captain was to engage the enemy unless it was absolutely necessary. American leaders were sure that attacking the British would be costly and useless and preferred to save as many ships as possible to defend the coastal cities. But Hull and his fellow captains had no intention of waiting for the British to come to them. For years, the Americans had endured insult after insult by British ships. U.S. captains felt it was now time to even the score.

During the last days of June 1812, Isaac Hull carefully prepared his ship for departure. He was nothing like his uncle, the inept William Hull, who was at that moment organizing his troops for the ill-fated trek to Detroit. The younger Hull was a talented, experienced seaman. He had served on several ships and fought in many battles since going to sea at the age of fourteen. With a watchful eye, Hull checked every supply list during the loading of the forty-four-gun *Constitution.* His 450-man crew included several marines who were expert shots with muskets, which were to be used if they came close enough to an enemy ship. Most crew members were new recruits who had never been on a large warship, so Hull trained and drilled them almost day and night. At noon on July 4, 1812, in honor of the nation's thirty-sixth birthday, the ship fired a fifteen-gun salute. The next day, it sailed from Annapolis for a date with destiny.

At about 2:00 P.M. on July 16, Hull's lookout sighted several sails on the horizon. At such a great distance, there was no way to tell whether they were American or enemy ships. Hull steered directly for the vessels in an attempt to identify them. By 5:00 the next morning, there was no longer any doubt. Five British warships were closing in at top speed on Hull's vessel. There were four frigates, the *Shannon, Belvidera, Aeolus,* and *Guerriere,* along with the sixty-four-gun ship of the line *Africa.* Hull believed that the *Constitution* was a match for any ship in single

The Death of Captain Lawrence

Thirty-two-year-old Capt. James Lawrence was one of the young American naval commanders who bravely challenged and engaged the mighty British navy during the War of 1812. Lawrence became a sailor in the late 1790s. He earned several promotions during a series of clashes between American ships and pirates from North Africa. When war broke out with Britain in 1812, Lawrence received command of the eighteen-gun USS *Hornet*. In February 1813, the *Hornet* fought and defeated the British sixteen-gun *Peacock*. This established Lawrence as a naval hero, and he became as famous and respected as Isaac Hull of the *Constitution* and Stephen Decatur of the *United States*.

A few weeks later, Lawrence was given command of a much larger ship. In May 1813, the *Chesapeake* was moored in Boston Harbor, where Lawrence readied it for combat. Although it was built to carry thirty-eight cannons, Lawrence added twelve more big guns and the extra crewmen to operate them.

While he was training his inexperienced crew, Lawrence received a challenge from Capt. Philip Broke of the British frigate *Shannon*. Broke had anchored his ship several miles outside of Boston Harbor in an attempt to block American shipping from getting in or out. Broke asked if Lawrence had the nerve to meet him "ship to ship, to try the fortunes of our respective flags." Although his crew was not yet fully prepared, Lawrence rashly sailed from Boston on June 1, 1813, to meet Broke's challenge.

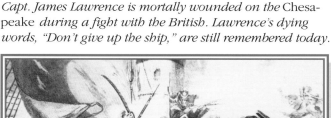

Capt. James Lawrence is mortally wounded on the Chesapeake *during a fight with the British. Lawrence's dying words, "Don't give up the ship," are still remembered today.*

In the late afternoon, the two ships approached each other and both immediately opened fire. Lawrence and his men fought valiantly, but Broke's better-trained gunners quickly gained the advantage. Fifteen minutes later, the *Chesapeake* was badly damaged and Lawrence mortally wounded. As he died, Lawrence gasped, "Don't give up the ship! Fight her till she sinks." The British soon boarded and captured the *Chesapeake,* but Lawrence's defiant final words became an inspiration to other U.S. naval commanders. Oliver Perry carried a flag bearing these words during his great victory on Lake Erie a few months later. And "Don't Give Up the Ship" became the proud motto of the U.S. Navy.

The Constitution *escapes from the British squadron after a chase lasting more than sixty hours.*

combat. But he realized that facing five ships was suicide. He could not risk allowing the United States to lose one of its best warships. There was no choice but to make a run for it.

The Great Chase

Hull decided that if he had to retreat, he would withdraw fighting. He had part of the stern, or back, rail cut away from the ship and mounted one of his biggest cannons there, facing his rear. He also ordered some sailors to widen the portholes in his rear-facing cabin and to poke cannons through the openings.

Less than an hour after the *Constitution* turned to flee, the wind suddenly died down. With the enemy ships closing in to within twelve miles, the American frigate was dead in the water. Without hesitation, Hull ordered some of the cutters, or rowboats, lowered. After attaching ropes to the front of the ship, sailors in the cutters began to row with all their might, dragging the *Constitution* forward. A few minutes later, Hull observed the enemy ships through his telescope. The *Belvidera* and *Shannon* had also lowered cutters to tow clear of the calm area.

At 7:00 A.M., it was obvious that the British, with more cutters in the water, were quickly gaining on the American ship. In desperation, Hull now ordered his men to start kedging. Six sailors jumped into a cutter and, their muscles straining, rowed a forty-seven-hundred-pound kedge, or anchor, far out in front of the ship. After they dropped the anchor into the water, sailors aboard ship began turning the capstan, the round spool holding

Isaac Hull

One of the finest American ship captains of the War of 1812, Isaac Hull (1773-1843) went to sea as a cabin boy at the age of fourteen. He gained command of a small ship when he was only nineteen and fought against pirates in the Caribbean Sea. In 1798, Hull was commissioned as a fourth lieutenant on the USS *Constitution*. When the United States fought the Barbary pirates of North Africa in the early 1800s, Hull commanded the small warship *Argus*. In 1806, Hull received a promotion to the rank of captain and in 1810 became commander of the *Constitution*.

During the War of 1812, Hull played a major role in two of the most important events in U.S. naval history. In the first, Hull's *Constitution* successfully outran a squadron of British warships during a grueling three-day chase. In the second, the *Constitution* defeated and sank the British frigate *Guerriere*. Both incidents united the American people behind the war effort and destroyed the belief that the British navy was unbeatable.

After the war, Hull continued to play a key role in naval affairs. For several years, he served as a naval commissioner, deciding on important naval policies. From 1824 to 1827, he commanded the U.S. Pacific Fleet, and from 1839 to his death in 1843, he led U.S. naval forces in the Mediterranean Sea.

During the War of 1812, Isaac Hull was one of a few key naval commanders who managed to disprove the common notion that the British navy was unbeatable.

the anchor cable, in order to haul in the cable. As they did, the ship inched forward toward the heavy anchor. Meanwhile, men in a second cutter rushed to drop another kedge farther forward, and the process was repeated.

At 7:30, with the *Belvidera* closing to less than half a mile, Hull hoisted the American flag and ordered the rear cannon to open fire. Although the shot fell short, the British rowers became wary and temporarily slowed down. But the *Shannon* pressed on, and the *Guerriere* swung wide to attack the *Constitution* from the side. Meanwhile, the huge battleship *Africa* loomed ever closer. Soon, the British transferred cutters from the *Aeolus* to the *Belvidera* and *Shannon*. The extra rowers further increased the speed of the two lead ships.

By 9:00, the *Belvidera* was within firing distance and its bow, or front, cannon blazed. A shout of defiance went up from the American sailors as the shots skimmed the water just short of the *Constitution*'s stern. The American frigate's cannons answered with a roar, one cannonball smashing into the *Belvidera*'s main deck. Next, the *Guerriere* opened fire, but its shots, like those of its sister ship, fell short.

The grueling towing and kedging dragged on until 11:00 A.M., when a breeze finally blew up. Hull ordered extra sail raised, and the *Constitution* suddenly sped forward, overtaking its own cutters. But the British now had the advantage of the wind as well, and the chase continued into the afternoon. Hull ordered most of the drinking water, twenty-three hundred gallons of it, thrown overboard in order to lighten the ship. This helped, and the gap between the *Constitution* and its pursuers widened from half a mile to nearly two miles.

Later that day and all through the night, the wind periodically appeared and disappeared. Hour after hour, exhausted men from both navies rowed until their muscles cramped, many catching short naps as they sat upright in the tiny cutters. Isaac Hull refused to leave his command post on deck and occasionally even helped his men turn the backbreaking capstan.

At dawn, Hull saw that the tireless efforts of his crew had maintained the ship's two-mile lead. An hour later, the wind increased, and the *Constitution* gained a burst of speed. The *Guerriere* and *Aeolus* attempted to sail landward to cut off the Americans' escape route to the coast. But the *Constitution*'s speed and some clever maneuvering by Hull foiled that plan, and the gap between the Americans and British continued to widen.

The chase continued well into the afternoon of July 19, at which point Hull could make out only one of the enemy warships trailing far behind. Finally, the British, angry and exhausted, gave up and turned away. As a gesture of respect, the entire crew of the *Constitution* stood at attention as Hull, who had not slept in more than three days, made his way toward his cabin. As he was about to go below, one crewman thanked Hull "for bringing us through alive and in one piece." In the words of a later captain of the *Constitution*, "Isaac Hull and his crew, who had been together at sea for just…[a few] days, had outsailed a numerically superior British squadron in a 57-hour demonstration of endurance, teamwork, and skilled seamanship. It would not be the last time that this combination would embarrass their English cousins."

Answering the Challenge

The *Constitution*'s successful evasion of the British squadron seemed to prove what American naval officers had been saying for a long time. U.S. officers and seamen were just as skilled as their British counterparts. Encouraged and emboldened by Hull's demonstration, American warships now stepped up their attacks on British shipping. The U.S. frigates *President, United States,* and *Congress,* as well as smaller warships like the *Hornet* and *Argus,* intercepted many British cargo ships attempting to get through to Canada.

But the British remained unimpressed by the "Yankee upstarts" who dared to challenge their mastery of the sea. Capt. James Dacres of the British *Guerriere* publicly scoffed at the American navy. He said the escape of the *Constitution* was a lucky break and issued an open challenge to any American ship to come out and fight him. His ship, he boasted, would quickly send any U.S. frigate to the bottom of the sea.

Isaac Hull, overseeing the *Constitution*'s resupplying in Boston, was eager to answer Dacres's challenge. Hull sailed from

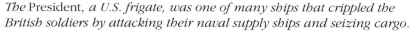

The President, *a U.S. frigate, was one of many ships that crippled the British soldiers by attacking their naval supply ships and seizing cargo.*

The battle between the American ship Constitution *and the British ship* Guerriere *ended in a dramatic victory for the Americans.*

Boston on August 2, 1812, and managed to capture three British cargo ships in the following two weeks. All the while, he searched for the *Guerriere,* which he knew was somewhere in the area. On August 19, at about 2:00 P.M. Hull's men spotted a sail several miles to the south. As the ships neared each other, Hull and his officers tensed with excitement. The British frigate bearing down upon them was none other than the *Guerriere.* Captain Dacres recognized the *Constitution* and informed his crew that the American ship could not be allowed to escape this time.

Immediately, both captains tried to position their ships for the "weather gauge," which was a strategic position gained by moving behind the enemy vessel while keeping one's own sails in the wind. A ship that gained this advantage could turn sideways and fire its cannons at the enemy's undefended stern. For forty-five minutes, Hull and Dacres moved around each other. Each displayed amazing skill, and neither could outmaneuver the other. Dacres fired the cannon on his port, or left side, but the shots fell short. A few minutes later, he tried again, and this time the cannonballs whizzed high over the *Constitution*'s masts.

In the meantime, Hull had spun his ship around. In a sudden surprise maneuver, he sailed directly toward the front of the British frigate. His intention was to veer off at the last moment and fire his cannon as he moved by the other ship. As the *Constitution* closed in, the American sailors begged three times to be allowed to shoot. Each time Hull ordered them to wait. Dacres tried desperately to pull away for he knew his ship would soon be wide open to the American guns. But he waited too long. A few seconds later, Hull ordered the jib sail lowered, slowing down the *Constitution* and bringing it within fifty feet of the enemy. "Now boys, pour it into them!" Hull screamed, and the American gunners opened fire with a vengeance. Blast after blast

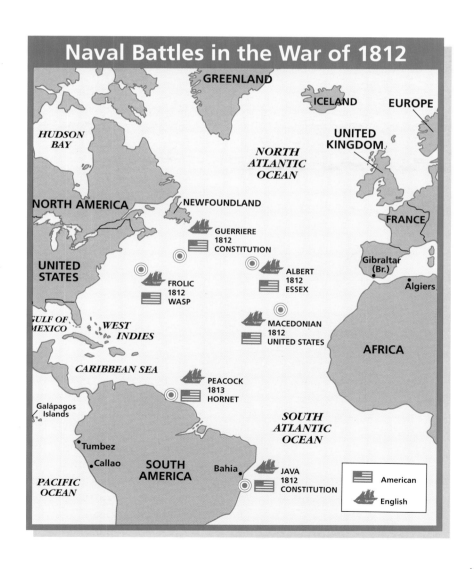

Naval Battles in the War of 1812

Old Ironsides

The USS *Constitution* is the most famous ship in the history of the American navy. The vessel earned the nickname "Old Ironsides" during its classic battle with the British warship *Guerriere* in the war of 1812. During the encounter, the British cannonballs seemed to bounce off the *Constitution*'s sturdy oak hull. The *Constitution,* designed by Joshua Humphreys, was one of the first three war frigates built for the U.S. Navy. Work began on the ship in 1794 in Boston and the vessel was launched in 1797. Constructed of live oak, red cedar, and hard pine, it was 204 feet long and weighed 2,200 tons. Famed patriot and silversmith Paul Revere crafted the copper sheathing on the ship's bottom. The vessel's design called for forty-four cannons with ranges of up to 1,200 yards each and it carried a crew of 450 sailors. Total cost of the *Constitution* in 1797 was $302,718.

After seeing action against the French (1797-1798), and North African pirates (1801-1805), the *Constitution* earned eternal glory for its exploits in the War of 1812. In addition to defeating the *Guerriere,* the U.S. frigate successfully outran five British warships and sank several others. By 1828, the navy was about to dismantle the aging *Constitution*. But public sentiment saved the ship and it was carefully restored. In the 1900s, it sailed to more than one hundred U.S. ports, where millions of people visited and toured it. Permanently docked in Boston, Old Ironsides remains a commissioned vessel in the U.S. fleet.

The Constitution, *nicknamed "Old Ironsides," seemed invincible. By the end of the War of 1812, the* Constitution *had successfully outrun five British warships and sank several others.*

hit the *Guerriere,* tearing rigging and sails to pieces. Hull jumped up and down, excitedly cheering on his gunners. The British gunners tried to return fire, but most of their shots missed. The ones that found their mark had little effect. According to both American and British eyewitnesses, several British cannonballs harmlessly bounced off the hard wooden hull of the *Constitution*. "Her sides are made of iron!" exclaimed an American sailor, which earned the ship its nickname of Old Ironsides.

After pounding the *Guerriere* until the rear mast split and fell into the water, Hull turned his own ship around. He now began to rake the British ship with fire, moving straight across its bow. This devastating maneuver allowed the American gunners located along the length of the *Constitution* to blast away one after another as they passed the enemy. Only a handful of cannons in the front of the *Guerriere* were pointed in the right direction, leaving Dacres's ship nearly defenseless. As the American cannons fired, Hull's marine sharpshooters sprayed musket fire onto the decks of the enemy ship.

A minute later, the wind shifted and the ships drifted dangerously close to each other. Before either captain could pull away, the bowsprit, or front mast, of the *Guerriere* became tangled in the *Constitution*'s rigging. The two ships were now attached to each other. Boarding parties from both ships surged forward. The American assault was led by Lts. Charles Morris and William Bush. Bush received a shot directly in the face as musket fire tore open Morris's stomach. Sailors with swords slashed at each other, while the ships heaved up and down and streams of blood flowed across the decks. Several British officers died in the fighting. After a few minutes, the ships drifted apart and Hull ordered his marines to open fire once more. Bodies plunged over the *Guerriere*'s railings and disappeared beneath the waves.

Less than two hours after the fight began, Captain Dacres, now wounded and humbled, fired a surrender shot and lowered his flag. The *Guerriere* was a helpless wreck. Twenty-three British were dead, and fifty-six were wounded. American losses were fewer, with only seven dead and seven wounded. Hull took the British survivors prisoner and ordered the remains of the enemy ship blown up. Captain Dacres stood in silence beside Hull as the British ship was destroyed. One of the American officers described the *Guerriere*'s end at 3:15 P.M., on August 20, 1812:

> There was a…shuddering motion, and streams of light, like streaks of lightning running along the sides; and the grand crash came! The quarterdeck…lifted in a mass, broke into fragments, and flew in every direction. The hull, parted in the center by the shock…reeled, staggered, plunged forward a few feet, and sank out of sight. It was a grand and awful scene.

A Beacon of Hope

Hull's victory marked the first time that an American ship had defeated a British warship. Hull and his crew shattered the myth of the invincibility of the British navy. One American politician commented that the battle had instantly raised the United States to the rank of a first-class naval power. There were celebrations in every American city, and Hull was hailed as a hero. By contrast, the British were shocked and bewildered. The London *Times* reported, "The loss of the *Guerriere* spread a degree of gloom through the town which it was painful to observe." According to the newspaper, the British

Hull's victory over the Guerriere *was the first time an American ship had beaten a British ship. The victory was hailed in American newspapers and lent new enthusiasm to the war effort.*

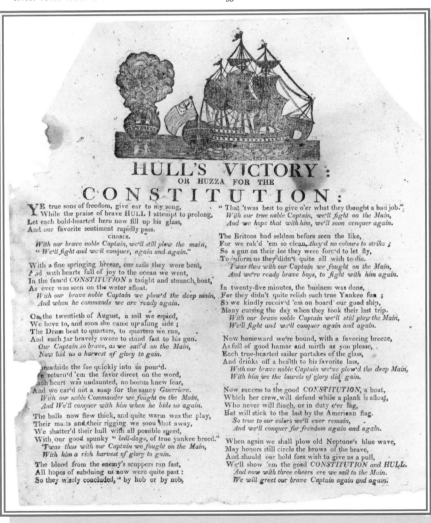

The United States, *piloted by commander Stephen Decatur, seizes the British frigate* Macedonian *after crippling it in battle.*

Naval commander Stephen Decatur won a stunning victory against the British when he seized the Macedonian.

ship had fallen to "a new enemy, an enemy unaccustomed to such triumphs and likely to be rendered…confident by them…. Above all, there is one object to which our most strenuous efforts should be directed—the entire annihilation of the American Navy."

Fulfilling this prediction, the American sea captains became more confident than ever. They quickly followed up Hull's triumph with more victories on the open sea. On October 18, 1812, the USS *Wasp* defeated the British *Frolic*. And on October 25, the *Constitution*'s sister ship, the *United States,* commanded by Stephen Decatur, mangled the British frigate *Macedonian*. In December 1812, Hull's own ship won another naval battle, this time destroying the frigate *Java*. The courage and skill of American seamen in the face of overwhelming odds became a source of pride and hope for the American people.

The British viewed the string of American victories with horror and disbelief. In late December, the *Times* asked in dismay, "What is wrong with British sea power?" The British promptly built new ships to replace those lost. Their image tarnished by defeat, the

The British frigate Java *is destroyed in a fiery explosion after doing battle with the USS* Constitution.

British officers gained respect for their American cousins but eagerly sought to soundly defeat them in future battles.

James Madison and other American leaders learned an important lesson about the importance of naval power. All agreed that the navy should be expanded as quickly as possible. But the country needed ships for more than just ocean warfare. There was still no American fleet at all on the Great Lakes. It was painfully clear that as long as the British controlled the lakes, the United States had no hope of winning the war.

CHAPTER FOUR

Battle for the Great Lakes

The lack of American warships and supply ships on Lakes Erie and Ontario put the United States at a severe disadvantage. During the disastrous Canadian campaign, the British commander Gen. Isaac Brock had shown the importance of controlling the lakes. He had used the vast system of connected lakes and rivers to move troops quickly from one place to another. He had also used these waterways to ferry a constant stream of weapons and supplies from the Atlantic coast. A steady supply of food from the East was essential. Thousands of British soldiers and their Indian allies had to be fed, and the undeveloped wilderness surrounding the Great Lakes provided little grain and cattle. As a result, there was simply no way to sustain large armies in the region without mastery of the lakes.

The importance of controlling the lakes became clear once again to the Americans during the winter of 1812 and 1813. William Henry Harrison had earlier halted his army south of Lake Erie when the fall rains made the wilderness impassable. Harrison's men were hungry and lacked supplies, including proper winter clothing. In January 1813, he ordered them to break camp and march north, hoping to retake Detroit, which had fallen to the British in the preceding summer. Harrison sent twelve hundred of his men up ahead to establish a base camp near Lake Erie. On January 22, they were surprised near the Raisin River by a force of British and Indians led by Gen. Henry Proctor, Brock's successor. Thanks to the British lakes fleet, Proctor was well supplied and his men were well fed. British ships helped move many of Proctor's troops within striking distance of the Americans. After

The Raisin River Massacre

Early in January 1813, William Henry Harrison's army was camped in the Ohio Valley. Harrison hoped to retake Fort Detroit, which had fallen to the British the year before. He sent a force of 1,200 men under Gen. James Winchester north to establish a base camp near the rapids of the Maumee River. Winchester reached the rapids on January 10 and began to set up camp. He then received an appeal for help from some American settlers in Frenchtown, thirty-five miles away on the Raisin River. The settlers said they were in danger of attack by Indians and British. Winchester sent 550 men, who secured Frenchtown on January 18. Two days later, Winchester arrived in the village with 300 more troops. Overconfident, he failed to erect proper defensive fortifications and posted no night guards.

On the night of January 21, Gen. Henry Proctor led a force of 1,200 British and Indians in a surprise attack on Winchester's camp. The Americans suffered heavy casualties, and Winchester surrendered. Proctor then ordered that most of the prisoners be robbed of their money, stripped of much of their clothing, and forced to pull British supply wagons. Proctor marched north, leaving the Indians in charge of the American wounded. Less than an hour later, the Indians massacred the helpless troops, scalping some, and herding the others into a flaming building. The incident became a rallying cry for the rest of Harrison's troops when they later confronted Proctor's forces on the Thames River.

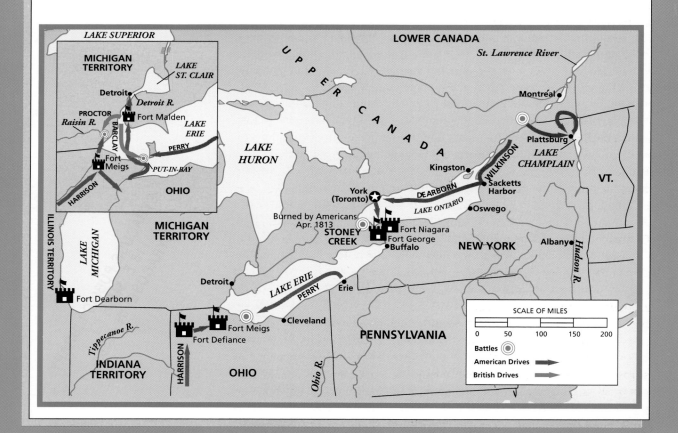

the Americans surrendered, the Indians massacred the survivors. The lack of supplies and the winter cold then took their toll on the rest of Harrison's army. His expedition ended in failure a few weeks later, largely because the British controlled the lakes and the major supply lines.

Building the U.S. Lakes Fleet

President Madison became determined to eliminate the British lakes fleet and gain control of the northwestern frontier. He put Commodore Isaac Chauncey of the New York Navy Yard in charge of creating and commanding an American fleet on Lakes Erie and Ontario. Late in 1812, Chauncey began establishing supply bases near the eastern shores of the lakes. He bought several small lake craft in the East and had them transported overland to his bases. There, they were refitted and converted into fighting vessels. He also brought green timber, miles of cord, cartloads of canvas, and dozens of cannons from the East. With these materials, he hoped to build several more ships, including at least two small frigates. What he lacked was the right man to oversee the building of the new ships and to train the crews.

In the last weeks of 1812, twenty-eight-year-old Comdr. Oliver Hazard Perry wrote to Chauncey and offered to build and command the new ships. Perry, who had gone to sea at the age of eleven, °was a gifted sailor and effective leader. Chauncey was delighted, writing back, "You are just the man I have been looking for." Perry arrived at Presque Isle, the future site of the city of Erie, located on the southern shore of Lake Erie, in March 1813. There, he took over the American shipbuilding operation. By April, six ships were under construction: two twenty-gun vessels and four smaller gunboats with two to four cannons each. Perry realized that these six ships were not enough to defeat the British. He desperately needed five of Chauncey's ships that were stationed at Black Rock on the Niagara River, between Lakes Erie and Ontario. Unfortunately, the British fleet, commanded by Capt. Robert Barclay, had the area blockaded. Chauncey's ships were trapped.

But Barclay also faced serious problems. He had only five ships: the *Lady Charlotte,* with eighteen guns; the *Lady Prevost,* with twelve guns; and three smaller gunboats. The twenty-gun *Detroit* was under construction near Fort Malden. This small fleet had been more than ample to control Lake Erie when the Americans had no fleet of their own. But soon, Barclay realized, Perry's ships would be completed. If Perry's group could link up with the ships at Black Rock, the British would be badly outnumbered and outgunned. Barclay also faced increasing supply and manpower problems. Most of the supplies that came from the East went to the British and Indian land troops, and his sailors had to make do

The Great Lakes System

In the 1700s and early 1800s, the term Great Lakes referred mainly to Lakes Erie and Ontario, and included the numerous rivers that flow from and into them. These lakes and rivers form a huge system of interconnected waterways that stretch from Detroit, on the western shore of Lake Erie, all the way to the Atlantic Ocean. Using the Great Lakes system, the British were able to transport troops and supplies into Canada and the American frontier almost completely over water. The people who settled the area wanted to be as close as possible to these reliable supply routes. Therefore, most of the original Canadian forts and towns were clustered around the Great Lakes system. These settlements included Detroit, Toronto, Montreal, and Quebec.

In order to reach Detroit from the Atlantic in 1812, people sailed into the Gulf of St. Lawrence north of Nova Scotia. This 200-mile-wide bay leads to the St. Lawrence River, which stretches southwestward for some 760 miles. At the head of the St. Lawrence, the ship entered Lake Ontario, which averages 800 feet in depth and covers more than 7,500 square miles. After sailing more than 150 miles across the lake, the ship entered the Niagara River. At Niagara Falls, where the land rises nearly 200 feet, the people crossed overland to another ship upriver from the falls. They then continued along the river to Lake Erie, about 210 feet deep with an area of over 9,900 square miles. After a journey of about 200 miles across that lake, the ship finally reached Detroit.

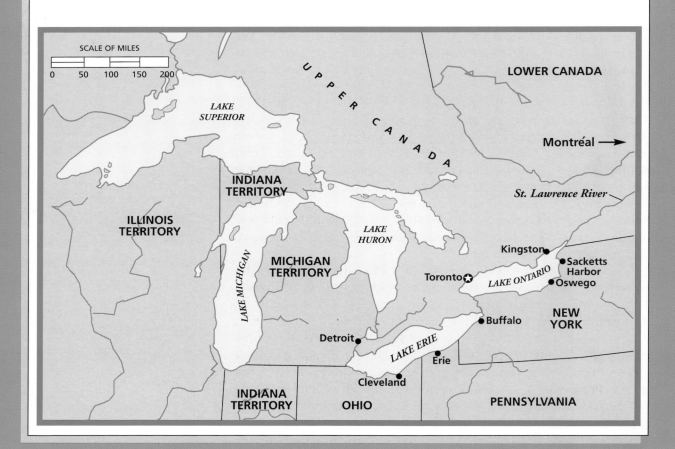

with what was left. Even worse, he did not have enough men and cannons to adequately outfit his new flagship, the *Detroit*.

In late May 1813, the military situation in the area changed. American troops moved into the Niagara region, forcing Barclay to lift his blockade against Black Rock. Chauncey's five ships were now free for service, and Perry promptly sent officers to sail them to Presque Isle. These vessels were moored in a small bay where they could be adequately guarded against British attack. At the same time, William Henry Harrison arrived in the Lake Erie region with another army. When Harrison did not immediately move on Fort Malden, Barclay realized Harrison was waiting for Perry to complete the U.S. fleet and engage the British.

Barclay decided that his best chance to defeat Perry was to take the British fleet to Presque Isle and try to destroy the American fleet before it was completed. When he approached the American base in June, however, he found the harbor blocked by a wide, submerged sandbar. Unable to get his ships close enough to fire on the Americans, Barclay anchored his fleet and blockaded the harbor. He wanted to launch a land attack against the American base, but he barely had enough sailors to man his own ships and Perry's position was too well defended. Barclay decided that waiting was the best strategy. He knew that Perry would have to drag the newly built American ships across the bar in order to get them out on the lake. During this operation, the vessels would be helpless and Barclay would be able to move in and destroy them.

Perry Crosses the Bar

On July 12, 1813, as his ships neared completion, Oliver Perry received horrible news. The British frigate *Shannon* had defeated the American frigate *Chesapeake* off the coast of Massachusetts in early June. The *Chesapeake*'s commander, Capt. James Lawrence, whom Perry greatly admired, had died in the battle. Lawrence's last words—"Don't give up the ship!"—moved and inspired Perry. He had a blue flag made, one similar in style to Lawrence's own, and ordered Lawrence's dying words sewn onto it. He hoisted it above his new flagship, which he officially christened the *Lawrence*. He named the other new twenty-gun vessel *Niagara*.

A few days later, Perry received orders from Chauncey to sail out onto the lake and attack the British. But Perry had two major problems. First, he did not have enough men to properly operate his ships. Second, Barclay's ships still guarded the sandbar. How could Perry be expected to launch an attack under these conditions? Perry wrote to Chauncey, begging, "For God's sake, and yours and mine, send me men." Chauncey could spare only sixty men, mostly sick or inexperienced. Desperate, Perry combed the countryside, offering any farmers and woodsmen he could find

British officers, seamen, and marines from the British frigate Shannon *board the* Chesapeake *and haul down the Stars and Stripes.*

ten dollars each to serve on his ships for four months. By the end of July, Perry was frantic. He had managed to scrape together only three hundred men, fewer than he needed, and in the meantime Barclay had launched the *Detroit,* armed with twenty cannons. The British clearly had the advantage.

Then, quite suddenly, the situation changed in Perry's favor. On August 1, 1813, the Americans awoke to find that Barclay's fleet had left during the night. Perry was dumbfounded. The only explanation he could think of for Barclay's departure was that perhaps one of the British forts was under attack and needed the support of the fleet. But in reality, the British withdrawal was the result of a combination of supply problems and poor planning. Barclay had not brought sufficient provisions for a lengthy blockade and finally had no choice but to withdraw to Fort Malden. This strategic blunder would cost the British dearly.

Perry wasted no time in taking advantage of the situation. He ordered every able-bodied person in the area to help get the ships over the sandbar. They towed the vessels out into the harbor until they were near the bar, which lay about four feet below the surface. Gangs of sailors brought in "camels," large hollow floats topped by decks of wood. First, the workers filled the floats with water so that they sank down beneath the level of the ships' portholes. Then, they ran long timbers through the ships' portholes, allowing the ends of the timbers to rest on the decks of the camels. Next, the sailors drained the water from the camels, which rose and carried the ships upward in the process. As the ships floated high in the water, teams of sailors rowing cutters dragged them over the bar. Working day and night, Perry's teams were able to get all of the ships out onto the lake by August 5. By this time, Barclay was on his way back to resume the blockade. But it was too late. Seeing the new American fleet fully deployed, he dared not attack. Barclay returned once again to Fort Malden.

Combat for Control of the Lakes

Perry now enjoyed almost complete freedom to roam Lake Erie. He quickly established another base at Put-in-Bay, on the western shore of the lake, south of Fort Malden. On August 10, Chauncey sent him ninety more sailors, led by young Lt. Jesse Elliott. Perry placed Elliott in command of the *Niagara*. A few days later, General Harrison, camped south of the lake, sent Perry one hundred Kentucky sharpshooters, dressed in buckskins and carrying muskets. Although they had never served on a ship, Perry was an excellent teacher, and the men quickly mastered the basics of seamanship. With his ships afloat and his crews trained, Perry was eager to engage the enemy. His chance came on September 10, 1813.

All through August, General Proctor had urged Captain Barclay to leave Fort Malden and attack the Americans. Proctor reasoned that the more time Perry had to strengthen his fleet, the weaker the British position on the lake would become. On the sunny morning of September 10, Barclay reluctantly maneuvered his fleet toward the American squadron at Put-in-Bay. Excited at the prospect of battle, Perry decided that Elliott's *Niagara* would face the *Lady Charlotte,* while the *Lawrence* would do battle with the *Detroit.*

At first, the wind blew the British ships directly at Perry's fleet. But about 10:00 A.M., the wind shifted, allowing Perry to get the weather gauge and bear down on Barclay's fleet. At 11:45, the British opened fire on the approaching *Lawrence,* and the battle began. As the two flagships, *Detroit* and *Lawrence,* blasted away at each other, the smaller gunboats weaved in and out of the fray. The American gunboats *Ariel* and *Scorpion* continually crossed in front of the bows of the larger British ships, raking them with cannon fire. Meanwhile, the Kentucky marksmen on the American vessels showered musket fire onto the decks of the enemy ships. As planned, Elliott tried to engage the *Lady Charlotte,* but the British ship kept its distance.

Oliver Hazard Perry

Oliver Perry (1785-1819) became a national hero when he defeated the British fleet on Lake Erie on September 10, 1813. He went to sea at the age of eleven and became a midshipman when only fourteen. While still a teenager, the energetic and dashing Perry displayed his courage and intelligence during battles with the Barbary pirates of North Africa. He quickly moved up through the ranks.

When the War of 1812 began, Perry had command of a group of small gunboats on the Atlantic coast. He asked for and received command of the American shipbuilding operation on Lake Erie. Through his leadership abilities, imagination, and hard work, Perry was able to create a U.S. lake fleet in only a few months. Perry combed the countryside, employing every blacksmith, carpenter, and able-bodied worker he could find. After moving his ships across a sandbar, he attacked and defeated the British fleet commanded by Robert Barclay. This gave the Americans control of the Great Lakes.

Later, in 1814, Perry was stationed in Washington, D.C., when the British attacked the city. He and other American captains bravely attempted to drive off the British ships in Chesapeake Bay. But the American craft were too tiny and did not have enough guns to stand up to the British frigates. After the war, the government sent Perry to Venezuela in South America to negotiate for expanded U.S. commerce in that region. In 1819, while returning, he contracted yellow fever and died at the age of thirty-four.

Oliver Hazard Perry is credited with creating the U.S. lake fleet that took control of Lake Erie on September 10, 1813. It was Perry's leadership and determination that led to the successful defense of the Great Lakes.

In the Battle of Lake Erie, Oliver Perry took Capt. James Lawrence's dying words to never give up the ship to heart. In spite of close fighting and the loss of his ship, Perry went on to win a complete victory over the British.

At first, neither fleet gained a definite advantage. Then, shortly after 12:30 P.M., the *Lady Charlotte* broke away from the *Niagara* and joined the *Detroit* in its assault on the *Lawrence*. For some unknown reason, Elliott did not follow the *Lady Charlotte* and remained too far away to assist Perry. Seeing their chance to destroy Perry's lead ship, the British commanders moved in for the kill. Nearly all of the British vessels opened fire on the *Lawrence,* and by 1:30, Perry's ship had been shot nearly to pieces. More than 80 percent of the ship's crew members were dead. The vessel swayed and tilted helplessly in the water.

It appeared that the Americans had lost the battle. But Perry, perhaps remembering Lawrence's dying words, refused to admit defeat. He grabbed the blue flag, jumped into a cutter, and rowed toward the *Niagara,* which was finally headed in his direction. British gunboats chased him, firing both cannons and muskets at Perry's tiny craft. As cannonballs splashed only feet from his boat, Perry saw the American gunboats *Scorpion, Porcupine,* and *Tigress* speed to his rescue. They chased off the British vessels, while Perry climbed aboard and took charge of the *Niagara.*

The British were sure that once aboard the *Niagara,* Perry would turn tail and run, acknowledging a British victory. This would have been a relief, for the British fleet was in poor shape. Two of its ships were disabled and on fire. Most of the British officers had died in the furious exchanges of cannonballs and musket fire. And Captain Barclay was badly wounded. But Perry did not give up. Minutes later, to their surprise, the British saw the *Niagara,* accompanied by the American gunboats, bearing down on them at full speed. The British sailors gallantly tried to maneuver their ships away, but it was no use. The *Niagara,* with Perry screaming orders from the foredeck, savagely raked the remaining British vessels.

The Lakes in American Hands

At 3:00 P.M., the British lowered their flags, admitting defeat. Perry ran his flag back up the mast of the *Lawrence,* which brought a cheer from the exhausted American sailors. Losses were heavy on both sides. Of the twenty-seven American dead, twenty-two were from the *Lawrence.* Ninety-six Americans were

After abandoning the crippled Lawrence, *Oliver Perry and his remaining men row toward the* Niagara *to continue the Battle of Lake Erie.*

Oliver Perry's superior leadership abilities and his refusal to give up lent inspiration and determination to his men.

wounded. Forty-one British were killed, and ninety-four were wounded. Most of the British ships were beyond repair.

Perry still had one more task to perform. General Harrison, with a force of several thousand men, was waiting for word of the outcome of the lake battle. Harrison realized that if the Americans won control of the lakes, the land advantage in the war would shift in his favor. Perry's ships could then ferry Harrison's troops to any point in southern Canada and also keep his army well supplied. Perry pulled an old envelope from his pocket and scratched out a note for Harrison. A day later, one of Perry's men rode into Harrison's camp and handed the general the note. Harrison smiled broadly when he read Perry's simple but momentous message: "We have met the enemy and they are ours."

After Perry's victory, British control of the entire Lake Erie region suddenly collapsed. Proctor's supplies had nearly run out, and his troops, including the Indians and their families, were on the verge of starvation. Fort Malden was defenseless because Barclay had stripped it of its cannons for use on the *Detroit*. There was nothing left to do but abandon the lake forts and retreat overland toward British strongholds far to the East. But Proctor's evacuation was far too slow and disorganized. He did

After Perry's victory, pictured here, British control of the entire Lake Erie region collapsed.

not realize that Harrison's forces were already moving toward Fort Malden. Proctor also failed to anticipate the ferocity of the approaching American soldiers. For the first time in the war, U.S. ground troops were passionately motivated and spurred on by a single goal. The massacre of U.S. troops at the Raisin River was still fresh in their memory, and they wanted revenge.

CHAPTER FIVE

Combat on the Frontier

The American victory on Lake Erie changed the balance of power in the northwest region of the United States. The British lost their hold over the area and could no longer effectively supply their Indian allies. But the danger to American settlers was far from over. The hostile Indian tribes that had been influenced and supported by the British still posed a threat to many parts of the western and southern frontiers. Even as the British withdrew, many tribes continued to attack the Americans. The British hoped that these uprisings would divert American resources and manpower away from the larger struggle with British troops. The British badly needed this diversion. Most of their troops and resources had to be used in fighting France, and they could make only a limited commitment of men and arms to the American war.

In fighting back against the British-inspired Indians, the Americans had two goals. The most obvious was to defeat the Indians as part of the overall war effort against Britain. The other goal had important consequences and benefits for the future of the United States. Conquering the Indians along the frontier would ensure faster and easier expansion of American settlements into the western territories. Pushing the Indians from their land would help the country grow and prosper. Of course, it was inevitable that this policy would worsen relations between the whites and Indians. The war with Britain not only intensified American-Indian tensions and hatreds but also established a pattern in which the whites continued to take Indian lands as the country expanded westward.

Still, not all of the Indians were at war with the Americans. Some tribes, such as the Choctaw in Louisiana and Mississippi, actually helped the United States fight other Indians. A few tribes, like the Wyandot in the Great Lakes region, started out fighting the Americans, then switched sides and helped the United States. American troops referred to these as "friendly" Indians. The friendly Indians believed that the Americans would reward them by allowing them to keep their own hunting grounds. But eventually, even those Indians who helped the United States lost their lands as white civilization marched westward.

In 1812, there were few friendly Indians helping the Americans. Most of the Indians inhabiting the huge frontier stretching from Canada to the Gulf of Mexico opposed the United States. They were inspired by Tecumseh, the great Shawnee chief who wanted to keep the white settlers from expanding any farther west.

Broken Promises and Retreat

Tecumseh was Britain's closest and most powerful Indian ally. He and his people were camped near Fort Malden while Oliver Perry and Robert Barclay battled for mastery of Lake Erie. Although they were too far away from the fighting to see the ships, the Indians could hear the thunder of the cannons in the distance. Tecumseh was aware that the British considered controlling the lakes their top priority. But he was more interested in fighting the Americans on land. In Tecumseh's view, it was land, specifically Indian land, that was at stake. The British had promised to help fight for that land, so Tecumseh was surprised when, following the lake battle, the British hastily prepared to abandon Fort Malden.

As General Proctor packed his personal belongings, Tecumseh confronted him. The chief demanded to know why the British were leaving. Would they abandon the Indians so easily after losing only one battle? "You told us," said Tecumseh, "to bring forward our families to this place and we did so. And you promised to take care of them and they should want for nothing while the men would go and fight the enemy; that we need not trouble ourselves about the enemy's garrisons [forts]...that our father would attend to that part of the business.... Our ships have gone one way and we are very much astonished to see our father tying up everything and preparing to run [the other way]."

The chief was clearly upset, and Proctor was worried because he desperately needed Tecumseh and his warriors to help protect the British retreat. If the chief thought the British were cowards, he might turn his back on his white allies. As Proctor feared, the charge of cowardice came next. "You always told us," said Tecumseh, "you would never draw your foot off British [and Indian] ground but now, Father, we see that you are drawing back and we are sorry to see our father doing so

The Custom of Scalping

Scalping, the removal of part or all of the scalp along with the hair, was commonly practiced by North American Indians in frontier warfare. Many white trappers and frontiersmen also scalped their enemies. Most American Indian tribes took scalps, but the custom was most widespread among the eastern and southern Indians. For example, the Creek and Choctaw, who inhabited the lands bordering the Gulf of Mexico, considered scalping an essential part of warfare. They believed that a young man had to take a scalp in order to become a full-fledged warrior. They also believed that the spirits of their ancestors could not rest in peace unless enemy scalps adorned their lodges. Most tribes of the midwestern plains considered scalping less important. They believed that stealing an enemy's horse or touching an enemy's living body were better tests for warriors because these acts took more courage. When they did take scalps, they often used them to decorate their clothing, weapons, or horses.

The practice of scalping became much more widespread among the Indians in the 1700s because of the influence of white European settlers. The whites introduced firearms, which caused more deaths and, therefore, more opportunities for scalping. The whites also introduced metal knives, which made scalping easier and more efficient. In addition, the French, Spanish, British, and Dutch all offered bounties of money or other valuables to Indians in exchange for scalps of both Indian and white enemies.

In this illustration, two Indians prepare to scalp a white pioneer woman.

without seeing the enemy. We must compare our father's conduct to a fat dog that carries its tail on its back, but when affrighted, drops it between its legs and runs off."

Luckily for Proctor, several of Tecumseh's fellow chiefs convinced him not to abandon the British. The Indians had given the British their word, said the chiefs, and it would be wrong to break a promise. Proctor assured Tecumseh that his warriors would be able to fight the Americans later at a better time and place. So Tecumseh reluctantly ordered his people to dismantle their lodges and prepare to depart. He was bitter about making his people leave the hunting grounds of their ancestors after years of fighting. On September 23, 1813, Tecumseh and his people watched with great sadness as Proctor's men set fire to Fort Malden. This was done so that the Americans would not be able to use the fort later. "We are now going to follow the British," Tecumseh said quietly, "and I feel certain that we shall never return." Great plumes of black smoke curled into the sky as some eight hundred British and twelve hundred Indians began their retreat northeastward toward the Thames River.

The Americans Give Chase

Unaware that the British were withdrawing, William Henry Harrison organized his men for an attack on Fort Malden. Harrison's army of five thousand joined forces with thirty-five hundred Kentucky riflemen under Gen. Isaac Shelby and one thousand cavalry, or soldiers mounted on horses, commanded by Col. Richard Johnson. Harrison ordered Johnson to ride his men around the lakeshore and move on the rear of Fort Malden. In the meantime, the rest of the army would take advantage of its new mastery of the lake. Harrison had Perry move his troops by ship to a point just south of Fort Malden. An operation that normally would have involved an overland trek of several weeks was completed in only a few days.

When the forces commanded by Johnson and Harrison converged on Fort Malden on September 26, they found a charred pile of rubble, parts of which were still smoldering. Harrison was encouraged rather than disappointed by the spectacle. Proctor's hasty retreat indicated that the British were in a weakened state and afraid of combat. Harrison rallied his forces and chased them. Johnson's cavalry crossed the Detroit River and galloped overland, while Perry's ships carried Harrison and a large part of his army farther along the lake toward the Thames River.

The British retreat was slow and poorly led. Proctor seemed more interested in his own needs and comfort than in the condition of his troops, and morale was low. Tecumseh's people told the chief there was no honor in this retreat. They said they would rather turn and face the Americans, no matter what the outcome.

William Henry Harrison

According to stories that were circulated when he ran for president in 1840, William Henry Harrison (1773–1841) was born in a humble frontier log cabin. But his real birthplace was a plantation mansion in Virginia. His father was the well-to-do Benjamin Harrison, a signer of the Declaration of Independence. As a young man, William Harrison studied medicine in Philadelphia. In 1791, he left school to pursue a military career. By 1797, he had risen to the rank of captain, and in 1800, President Jefferson appointed him governor of the newly created Indiana Territory. Harrison served in this post until war broke out with Britain in 1812.

In 1811, during his last year as governor, Harrison performed an act for which he would always be remembered. He led American troops against an Indian uprising commanded by the great Shawnee chief Tecumseh. But Tecumseh was away at the time, and Harrison managed to defeat only Tecumseh's incompetent brother. Nevertheless, the battle of Tippecanoe Creek made Harrison a national hero. During the War of 1812, he commanded all of the U.S. troops fighting in the northwestern frontier.

In later years, Harrison served as a congressman, a senator, and a U.S. ambassador. In 1840, the Whig party picked him as its presidential candidate, reminding voters of the victory at Tippecanoe in campaign slogans. He won the election at the age of sixty-seven but

During the War of 1812, William Henry Harrison commanded all of the U.S. troops in the northwestern frontier. He later became the ninth president of the United States.

died of pneumonia after serving only thirty-one days in the White House. His grandson Benjamin Harrison became the twenty-third U.S. president in 1889.

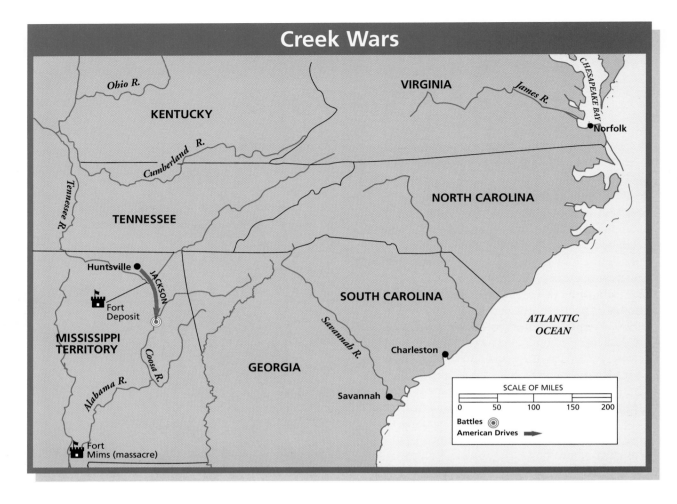

Creek Wars

On October 4, 1813, Tecumseh once again accused Proctor of cowardice, reminding him that the British had broken their promises to the Indians. The chief informed the British leader that they must now turn and make a stand against the Americans. Otherwise, the Indians would go no farther with the British. At the same time, Proctor received word that the Americans had captured his supply boats only a few miles to his rear and were approaching fast. Proctor realized he no longer had a choice. He would have to fight. With darkness setting in, he camped his forces beside the Thames, near the future site of Thamesville.

That night, Tecumseh sat silently beside his fire. A young warrior approached him and asked, "Father, what are we to do? Shall we fight the Americans?" Tecumseh nodded, saying, "Yes my son, on the morrow, we will be in their smoke [given off by their muskets]." The chief then gathered his people around him and announced, "My children, hear me well. Tomorrow we go to our final battle with the Americans. In this battle I will be killed." There was a gasp from the listeners. No one knew how the chief was able to predict his own death. But no one doubted the prediction. Their leader had correctly foreseen many victories and other happenings, and they accepted that he had a gift for seeing into the future.

"You are my friends, my people," Tecumseh continued. "I love you too well to see you sacrificed in an unequal contest from which no good can result…. Yet…you have made known to me that it is your desire to fight the Americans here and I am willing to go with my people and be guided by their wishes." Tecumseh then gave away all of his possessions to his family and friends, as was the custom of many Indians who knew they were dying. Afterward, he once more sat silently before the fire, and out of respect, no one disturbed him.

Slaughter on the Thames

On the morning of October 5, 1813, Proctor formed a defensive line near the river. On the left side of the line, he placed his British regulars and on the right Tecumseh's Indian forces. They watched the much larger American army approach to within several hundred yards. Shortly before noon, Harrison ordered Richard Johnson to charge his cavalry directly at the British regulars. Commander Perry, seemingly as much at home on a horse as on a ship, led one detachment. Screaming "Remember the Raisin River!" the cavalry quickly broke through the British lines. Most of Proctor's soldiers were able to fire only one shot. As they rushed to reload, Americans with pistols and tomahawks attacked them. The charge was so devastating that the British retreated in confusion. Only three of Johnson's one thousand men were wounded.

Gen. William Harrison confronts Tecumseh.

Richard Johnson (in foreground, mounted) charges his cavalry toward the Indian allies of the British. Vastly outnumbered, the Indian opposition quickly collapsed.

At the same time, Harrison moved forward with his foot soldiers. As they launched a frontal assault on the Indians, Johnson's horsemen swung around and attacked the Indians' rear. Tecumseh's warriors fought bravely, but they were hopelessly outnumbered. The great chief fell dead as a group of Americans emptied their muskets into the Indian ranks. Seconds later, Johnson was wounded and fell from his horse. As an Indian ran at him, tomahawk raised to strike, Johnson shot him through the forehead, then fell unconscious.

The battle that Harrison and his men had been waiting so long to fight lasted only five minutes. Seeing Tecumseh fall, the surviving Indians disappeared into the forest. Proctor ran from the field just after Johnson's cavalry broke through the British lines. The British later demoted Proctor in rank for his poor conduct during the retreat and battle. In this decisive U.S. victory, seven Americans died and twenty-two were wounded. They captured more than one million dollars' worth of weapons. The British had eighteen dead, twenty-five wounded, and more than six hundred captured. Only thirty-three Indian bodies were found, but Harrison was sure that the Indian survivors carried away many of their dead.

Immediately following the battle, a group of American soldiers searched the field for Tecumseh's body. They found Simon Kenton, an old frontier scout who had known Tecumseh well, and demanded that he identify the remains of the fallen chief. Kenton, who admired and respected Tecumseh, purposely pointed out the wrong body. The soldiers stripped the body, scalped it, then cut strips of skin from the arms, legs, cheeks, and other areas. They wanted to use the skin to make pouches and belts as souvenirs. Early the next morning while it was still dark, several Shawnee warriors recovered the body of the real Tecumseh. They carefully carried it to a secret spot deep in the forest and buried it. Then they sorrowfully chanted, "Tecumseh will come again…. The sign of his second coming will be a star appearing and passing across the sky…Tecumseh will be born again…for all Indians."

The Creek War

Buried with Tecumseh were his dreams for a federation of all frontier Indian tribes. But even in death, he remained an inspiration to many Indians who hated and distrusted the Americans. Many tribes followed his example and rose up against the whites in the following months. An uprising of the Creeks was the biggest and most famous. Though no British soldiers took part, the American struggle against the Creeks was an important episode in the war with Britain. The British and Tecumseh had inspired the Creeks, and the British later tried to forge an alliance with them against the Americans.

The Creeks inhabited large sections of Georgia, Alabama, and Florida. White settlers had been constantly pushing their way

Creeks overrun Fort Mims and massacre the whites who took refuge there. Of the more than five hundred soldiers and settlers in the fort, only a handful escaped.

Tecumseh

Tecumseh had seen his father and brothers killed by whites and much of his tribe's land taken over by them. His dream of an Indian alliance to stem the tide of whites died with him at the Battle of the Thames.

Born in what is now Ohio, Tecumseh (1768–1813) was the greatest Shawnee war leader. As a boy, he constantly witnessed fighting between his people and American settlers who poured into the Ohio Valley. Many of his relatives were killed by whites and he came to believe that the only way to stop the Americans was to unite all Indians against them. In 1795, Tecumseh broke with the other Shawnee chiefs who were attempting to negotiate with the Americans. He organized a band of followers and traveled around the frontier convincing other tribes to join him. During these journeys, he gained a reputation as a skilled leader and orator, and claimed to be able to foresee future events. One event he correctly foretold was that the whites would eventually take all Indian lands if the Indians did nothing.

As relations between the United States and Britain worsened in 1810, Tecumseh sought the help of the British. He hoped that a British-Indian alliance would defeat the Americans. He believed the British leaders who promised to support permanent Indian nations along the frontier. During the War of 1812, Tecumseh led his followers to a number of victories. Occasionally, in the absence of a British commander, he took charge of British troops. In 1813, after Oliver Perry defeated the British on Lake Erie, Tecumseh took part in the British retreat from Fort Malden. A few days later, he died at the Battle of the Thames north of the lake. The idea of Indian unity died with him.

During the War of 1812, Indians staged repeated surprise attacks on white settlements.

into Creek lands in Georgia since the days of the American Revolution. Tecumseh had visited the Creeks in 1811 and encouraged them to fight back against the Americans. After hearing of the British-Indian victories over the Americans during the fall and winter of 1812, the Creeks decided to take Tecumseh's advice. They launched attacks on many American settlements on the southern frontier. The worst and most publicized incident occurred on August 30, 1813. About one thousand Creeks overran Fort Mims, located about forty-five miles north of the town of Mobile on the Alabama River. Of the more than five hundred soldiers and settlers in the fort, only a handful escaped alive.

The American government reacted quickly to the Creek uprisings because the thousands of American settlers who lived in the southern states and territories had to be protected. Also, American leaders feared that the Creeks might join with other tribes along the coast of the Gulf of Mexico. The British would surely take advantage of this situation and ally themselves with the tribes. With thousands of Indians to support them, the British could more easily attack New Orleans and other towns on the gulf. President Madison asked Willie Blount, the governor of Tennessee, to raise an army to fight the Creeks. Blount picked Maj. Gen. Andrew Jackson of the Tennessee militia to lead the more than three thousand men who eagerly volunteered to fight. Jackson, a tall, imposing, and dynamic individual, had already gained fame as a local politician and Indian fighter.

Between November 1813 and March 1814, Jackson's forces repeatedly attacked and defeated the Creeks. The Indians offered tough, courageous resistance but were unable to defeat the Americans, who had more men and better weapons. In late March 1814, twelve hundred Creeks made a desperate last stand at Horseshoe Bend on the Tallapoosa River in Alabama. The Creeks tried to fortify a small peninsula jutting out into the river by piling up logs in

Sam Houston (top) and Davy Crockett were among the men in Andrew Jackson's army during the War of 1812.

front of their position. They placed their canoes along the riverbank to their rear in case escape became necessary.

Jackson approached Horseshoe Bend on the morning of March 27 with a force of more than three thousand, including more than two hundred friendly Cherokee. Among the Tennesseans were famed frontiersmen Sam Houston and Davy Crockett. Jackson ordered an immediate attack. As he led a frontal charge, the Cherokee swam the river and captured the Creek canoes. The Creeks were trapped on the peninsula, and the Americans closed in. After several hours of furious hand-to-hand combat, most of the Creek warriors lay dead. About 300 Creek women and children were taken prisoner. The Americans and Cherokee had 44 dead and 142 wounded.

There was some further scattered Creek resistance in the following months, but their cause was hopeless. In August 1814, they acknowledged defeat and gave up half of their lands, about twenty-three million acres, to the Americans. It was fortunate for the United States that Jackson was able to defeat the Creeks so quickly. As the Americans had feared, the British tried to join forces with and supply arms to the Creeks as part of a campaign against the southern United States. But it was not until midsummer of 1814 that the British began negotiating with the Indians. By that time, the Creeks were no longer a military threat, and British attempts to turn them into an effective fighting force failed.

American Hopes for Victory

By the spring of 1814, many Americans felt confident that they would triumph over the British in this war. U.S. forces had already won several dozen battles against the British and Indians in the northwestern and southern frontier regions. Most of the backwoods areas stretching from the Great Lakes south to Mississippi were once again under American control. Many settlers returned to their homes, and thousands more moved west to occupy the lands taken from the Indians.

Most of the Americans' successes were largely due to the efforts of young, effective leaders like Perry, Harrison, and Jackson. President Madison continued to replace the older, less competent generals with younger, more vigorous men. This improved the morale of the troops and inspired hopes of a speedy victory over the British.

But these hopes were short-lived. In April 1814, the British and their European allies decisively defeated Napoleon, finally bringing the long war with France to a close. The British could now devote many more troops, ships, and supplies to the American conflict. Before, the war with the United States had been only a minor diversion for the British. Now, the strongest nation on earth began making its plans for a full-scale invasion of the United States.

CHAPTER SIX

The Fall of Washington

The defeat of France changed the nature of the war between the United States and Great Britain. Although the Americans suffered several setbacks in the early months of the war, U.S. prospects improved markedly after that. For one thing, U.S. warships on the Atlantic coast performed splendidly once they began to battle the British ships. And the recent victories on the Great Lakes and along the frontier seemed to shift the tide of warfare in the Americans' favor. Many in the United States felt this proved they were a match for the arrogant British. But much of this recent success was the indirect result of Napoleon's efforts against the British. As long as they fought the French, the British were unable to devote adequate soldiers and supplies to the fight in North America. Now that the war in Europe was over, the British would be able to concentrate all their energies and resources against the United States.

This new turn of events greatly worried President Madison and other American leaders. They now realized that perhaps it had been foolish to pass up earlier opportunities to make peace with Britain. The first was in the summer of 1812. The U.S. government could have canceled its war declaration when the news came of the suspension of the Orders in Council. But the war hawks had insisted on fighting so that the country could attack and conquer Canada. That enterprise, however, was a dismal failure.

The second chance for peace came in early 1813 when the United States seemed to be winning the war. The British, still preoccupied with the French, seemed willing to negotiate. But the Americans stubbornly insisted that there could be no peace

The Fall of Washington   **75**

A NEW SONG,

ON THE DEATH OF ROBERT HOWEL.

ROBERT HOWEL, *an American citizen, pressed into the British service, and by Britons most* BARBAR-OUSLY MURDERED *on being compelled to fight on board the* Little Belt, *against his own countrymen, in which unnatural conflict he lost his leg and thigh, struck off by a cannon ball, and died in a few hours after, of the wound.*

I SAT where a precipice frown'd—
   All was still, save the wave's murm'ring flow,
And dark, save the sea that encompass'd me around,
   Held the moon in its bosom below.

There as musing dejected and lone,
   Bleeding country, thy wrongs were my care,
Tossing light, mid the billows, a form dimly shone,
   And, *Howel!* thy spirit was there!—

Uncoffin'd he burst on the view!
   Dark and harsh was his corse winding sheet,
And his corpse, pale and mangled, the bloody wave
      threw
   On the cold pointed rock at my feet!

Horror struck, not a breath could I draw!
   Not a word could my anguish declare—
But the dead from his rock rising slowly I saw,
   And his wound to my eyes he laid bare!

Then his hand waving soft, and his eye
   Wet so late with affections last tear,
Sparkling life—and his breast heaving deeply a sigh—
   Broke his rage kindling voice in my ear.

" Go, stranger, I bid thee go—
   Go and cry to the brave and the free—
Go and bid the heart's current more rapidly flow
   When they think of their brethren like me !

For myself, I would scorn to appeal—
   Ah! for me no appeal could avail!
But I weep, that my country too coldly should feel
   The wrongs which her children assail.

How long, and the nation still deaf,
   Shall the groans of her seamen resound!
To their shame, to their stripes, to their multiplied grief
   Is no end, but in death to be found!

By myself, dragg'd a slave from the shore,
   Where with friends and with home I was blest;
By this trunk wet and pale and with blood clotted o'er,
   By the deep, where it's doom is to rest.

Go and find me some Adams, to plead,
   Some Hancock to burn o'er the slain—
Again this cold fragment is welcome to bleed,
   If my country be *washed* by its slain !

Go, stranger, I bid thee to go—
   Go and cry to the brave and the free—
Go and bid the heart's current more rapidly flow
   When they think of their brethren like me !

He said, and the mist of the eve
   Veil'd his form, as it pass'd from my view;
And I vow'd, left in silence and sadness to grieve,
   To his charge, I'd be faithful and true.

FINIS

PRINTED and SOLD by N. COVERLY, Jun. Milk-street, Boston.

This poem was written to commemorate the death of Robert Howel, an American sailor impressed by the British and forced to fight against his countrymen. British impressment of American sailors remained a problem during the War of 1812.

unless the British first stopped impressing U.S. sailors. The British maintained that they had a right to impress Americans as long as the two countries were at war. If the Americans first agreed to stop fighting, British negotiators suggested, perhaps the British would stop impressing seamen. But the Americans refused to compromise on the matter.

Now, in 1814, with the United States facing Britain's full military strength, Madison did more than compromise. He withdrew his earlier demands. He sent negotiators to tell the British that he was dropping the impressment issue as a condition for peace.

But it was too late. The victory over Napoleon had given the British people new confidence. One of Madison's negotiators wrote home, "The whole nation is delirious with joy.... They thirst for great revenge and will not be satisfied without it." Many British citizens urged their government to teach the Americans a lesson once and for all. The British refused even to talk about bargaining. Realizing that they now had a huge military advantage, the British prepared to cross the Atlantic in full force and bring their former subjects back under British domination.

The British Invasion Plan

The new British strategy involved a three-pronged assault on the United States. The largest invasion force would move down Lake Champlain and attack New York State from the north. The object of this maneuver was to split the nation in half, separating New England from the rest of the country. The British were well aware that there was still a great deal of opposition to the war in New England, where many people considered the war, which they believed was unwinnable, to be a useless drain on American money and resources. For this reason, New England, the most prosperous section of the country, had not contributed its fair share of money to the war effort. Some states, such as Tennessee, had allowed detachments of their militia to fight in the regular army, but the New England states refused to call up their militia unless directly attacked. Many New Englanders continued to grumble about seceding from the Union. The British believed that once New York fell, the New England States could be convinced to join Britain. The other states could then be easily defeated.

The second British invasion would involve a combination of army and navy forces that would attack the largest U.S. coastal cities. The most important objective was the capital, Washington, D.C. Other cities targeted were Baltimore, Maryland; Charleston, South Carolina; and Savannah, Georgia. This operation would achieve two goals. First, it would divert U.S. troops and resources away from the New York assault. Second, the British believed that attacking major cities would frighten, dishearten, and embarrass the American people.

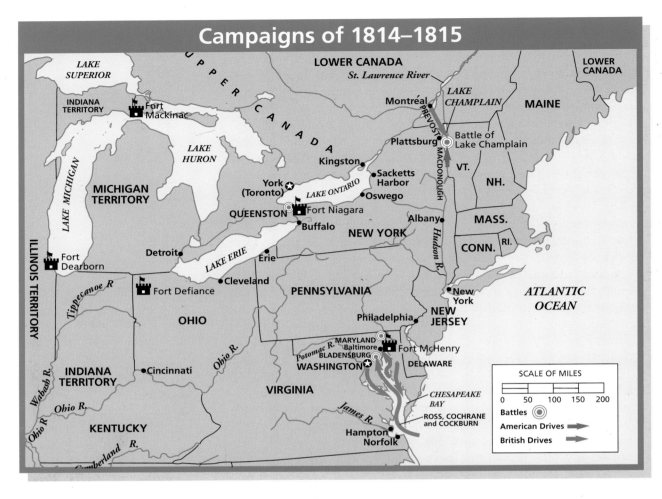

Campaigns of 1814–1815

The third British assault would be on the Gulf of Mexico coast, beginning with the largest and most important southern city—New Orleans. Located at the mouth of the Mississippi River, New Orleans was the key to control of river shipping. The British reasoned that capturing New Orleans would cut off all commerce moving north into the western frontier. There was an even more important strategic value to taking New Orleans. Commanding the Mississippi River would eventually give the British mastery of the vast regions of the Louisiana Purchase, through which the river flowed. Britain would then have a new foothold in North America, one rich in farmland, timber, furs, and other resources.

Out for Revenge

By July 1814, the British were nearly ready to put their grand invasion plan into effect. The army-navy assault on the coastal cities would move first, under the direction of Adm. Alexander Cochrane. At first, Cochrane planned only to capture the cities, not destroy them. But at the last minute, there was a change of plans. In mid-July, Cochrane received a letter from Gen. George Prevost, who was still in command of British forces in Canada. Prevost described how American troops had unnecessarily looted and burned some Canadian towns near Lake Erie. These actions had not been authorized by American commanders, who sent Prevost an apology. But because it took so long for the messenger to travel across the frontier, the apology arrived after Prevost had already written to Cochrane. Prevost asked his colleague to "assist in inflicting the measure of retaliation which shall deter the enemy from a repetition of similar outrages." Cochrane agreed to make his own operation, at least in part, a revenge raid. He informed his troops, "You are hereby required and directed to destroy and lay waste such towns and districts upon the coasts as you may find assailable [easy targets]."

In early August 1814, Cochrane's fleet arrived at Chesapeake Bay, the large waterway separating the coastal sections of Virginia and Maryland. Baltimore, one of the prime British targets, lay near the northern shore of the bay. Washington, another important target, lay between the Potomac and Patuxent rivers, both of which flow into the bay. Cochrane's forces were formidable, consisting of four huge ships of the line and twenty frigates and sloops. There were also twenty troop transport ships, carrying a total of more than four thousand battle-hardened British troops.

The only American ships defending Chesapeake Bay at the time were fifteen small gunboats commanded by Commodore Joshua Barney. Realizing his boats had no chance against the British fleet, Barney retreated up the Patuxent River. After conferring with his officers, Gen. Robert Ross and Adm. George Cockburn, Cochrane decided to chase and capture Barney's boats before attacking the cities. General Ross landed troops on the shore of the Patuxent. While Cochrane's ships pursued Barney along the river, Ross and his men marched ahead and placed themselves behind the American boats. By August 22, Barney was trapped. He blew up his gunboats rather than allow them to fall into British hands. The way was now clear for the British to attack either Washington or Baltimore, and they chose Washington.

Washington in Flames

The capital of the United States was nearly defenseless. The Americans had expected the British to strike at Baltimore first. So, U.S. commanders had failed to prepare adequate barricades and other defenses around the capital. There were fewer than two thousand soldiers available to defend Washington and its surrounding towns. Making matters worse, nearby states refused to send militia to the city. Located in the District of Columbia, which is a special federal

A map of the Battle of Bladensburg. The British had to pass through Bladensburg before they were able to attack the capital.

territory, Washington is not part of any state. Therefore, the governor of Maryland called out his militia to fortify Baltimore but would not approve troops for the U.S. capital. When Gen. William Winder, who was in charge of the defense of Washington, asked for three thousand troops from nearby states, he got only three hundred. President Madison then angrily issued an emergency order, and Maryland's governor reluctantly dispatched two thousand troops to Washington.

On August 23, 1814, British forces under General Ross marched westward from the Patuxent River toward Washington, about fifteen miles away. Hearing that the British were approaching, most of the citizens of the capital panicked. People fought over horses, wagons, and carts to carry them and their possessions out of the city. Many families boarded up their houses and buried their valuables before fleeing. Dolley Madison, the president's wife, tried to save some of the priceless objects in the

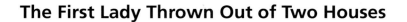

The First Lady Thrown Out of Two Houses

Dolley Madison (1768–1849), wife of President James Madison, was one of the most colorful and memorable first ladies. Known for her charm, wit, and skill as a hostess, she served as an unofficial first lady during the presidency of Thomas Jefferson, who was a widower. While her husband was Jefferson's secretary of state, she often helped the president entertain guests. When Madison became president in 1809, she increased the number and size of White House parties, and her fame as a hostess grew.

As British troops approached Washington on August 24, 1814, the president left his wife in charge of the White House, begging her to flee if the enemy entered the city. All through the day, she diligently packed important presidential papers as well as books, antiques, and the house silver. In the late afternoon, a hastily scribbled note arrived from Madison warning that the British would soon seize the city. The first lady insisted on staying long enough to rescue the famous portrait of George Washington painted by Gilbert Stuart.

Forced to leave her home, Dolley Madison hurried to meet her husband who had set up camp about sixteen miles away. She stopped at a farmhouse to rest, where she soon found out how much respect the president had lost in recent months. The lady of the house began screaming at her, "Your husband has got mine out fighting, and damn you, you shan't stay in my

First Lady Dolley Madison was known for her wit and charm. Madison was responsible for saving valuable articles from the White House before it was burned to the ground during the War of 1812.

house! So get out!" Humiliated, the first lady left. The perfect hostess had been forced out of two homes in one day.

White House. Among the art treasures she hurriedly packed was an original painting of George Washington.

Meanwhile, General Winder rushed all available soldiers to the nearby town of Bladensburg. The British would have to pass through this town in order to enter Washington. Madison and his cabinet members, including Secretary of State James Monroe, galloped into Bladensburg during the morning of August 24. They were ready to fight if needed. A few minutes later, the troops from Maryland arrived. The U.S. forces now numbered more than five thousand, which was one thousand more than the British. But the Americans, having rushed to the scene from every direction, were confused, disorganized, and exhausted.

At 1:00 P.M., the British attacked. At first, the American lines held firm. But then the British started firing Congreve rockets. These small projectiles, not much larger than ordinary fireworks, were practically harmless. The British expected the rockets only to frighten away some of the American horses and pack mules. The animals took flight all right, but so did most of the American troops, who thought the rockets were lethal. After only fifteen minutes of fighting, the bulk of the U.S. forces panicked and fled. One captain ran so hard and fast that he fell dead from exhaustion. Madison, Monroe, Winder, and the other American leaders knew that the rockets were harmless. But it was too late to stop the retreat of their troops. Madison and his cabinet had no choice but to join the mad flight, which many Americans later referred to unflatteringly as the "Bladensburg Races." The Americans did not stop running until they were sixteen miles from the capital. The city was now completely undefended.

That evening, General Ross and Admiral Cockburn led their troops into Washington, which was largely deserted. They immediately set fire to the U.S. Capitol Building, then made their way

The capture and burning of Washington by the British in 1814.

(above) Washington is set afire by the British under the leadership of General Ross. (right) After the fire, the Capitol lay in ruins.

through the silent streets to the White House. Dolley Madison and her servants were nowhere to be found, but it was obvious that they had fled only a short time before. The dining room table was set, and lamb, chicken, and vegetables were cooking in the kitchen. Pleasantly surprised by the scene, the British officers sat down and ate supper. Afterwards, they burned the White House and moved on.

In the next few hours, the British continued to burn and ransack the city. They torched the Navy Yard, the War and Treasury buildings, the Library of Congress, and the office of the city's largest newspaper, the *National Intelligencer.* The British burned houses and looted stores. From their position in the surrounding hills, American leaders, troops, and civilians watched the fire's flickering red glow dance against the clouds. Some swore angrily.

Congreve Rocket

During the 1600s, Europeans, including the French, Germans, and Poles were using rockets in battle. Most of these devices were small and posed no threat to soldiers except in the case of a direct hit. Since rockets were wildly inaccurate, there were few direct hits and they were not used very often. However, some generals used them to set fire to buildings or the sails of ships, and also to scare away horses and pack animals.

In the early 1790s, Haidar Ali, an Indian prince, invented a twelve-pound rocket with a range of one-and-a-half miles. He fired thousands of these weapons at the British in India, inflicting much fire damage and several casualties. Surprised and impressed, the British army officer William Congreve developed similar rockets which later bore his name. In a massed rocket attack in 1807, the British fired twenty-five thousand of the devices at Copenhagen, Denmark, burning the city to the ground. On August 24, 1814, the British, hoping to frighten U.S. pack mules, fired a few Congreve rockets at the Americans at Bladensburg. The terrified American soldiers fled, leaving Washington, D.C., open to British attack.

Others cried. All stood by feeling helpless as the enemy destroyed the national capital. That night, a violent thunderstorm put out the flames, but the damage had already been done. Washington was a pile of charred ruins.

By the Dawn's Early Light

After capturing and burning Washington so easily, the British were confident that they would have little trouble taking their next city—Baltimore. They expected to sail their warships into the harbor, which was protected by Fort McHenry. The ships would destroy Fort McHenry with cannon fire, then land troops for a frontal assault on the city. At the same time, Ross would lead his forces overland and attack the city from the rear. But this time, the British plan did not go so smoothly. Their assault on the capital had given the Americans time to properly fortify Baltimore, where sixteen thousand U.S. troops were concentrated. Aided by thousands of civilians, they built barricades and sank dozens of small ships to block the harbor.

The British moved on Baltimore on September 12, 1814. When Ross tried to attack by land, he was killed and the Americans drove back his troops. The British vessels entering the harbor could not get past the barrier of sunken ships. They bombarded Fort McHenry from a distance during the night of September 13. The British continuously launched rockets in order to illuminate the fort so their gunners could see what they were firing at. The gunners managed to lob more than eighteen hundred cannonballs into the small fort during the twenty-five-hour attack. A Washington lawyer named Francis Scott Key witnessed the bombardment from a boat about eight miles away. All through the night, he could see the fort's American flag lit up

The British hurl cannonballs at Fort McHenry. The bombardment, which lasted through the night of September 13, 1814, inspired Francis Scott Key to write "The Star-Spangled Banner."

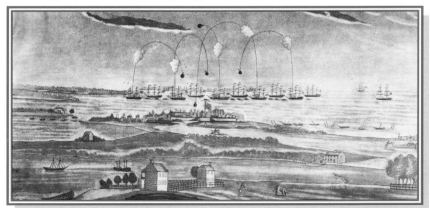

The National Anthem

On September 13, 1814, Britain's Admiral Cochrane began a naval bombardment of Fort McHenry, which guarded the approach to the city of Baltimore. Earlier that day, a Washington lawyer named Francis Scott Key had boarded one of the British ships. His mission was to negotiate the release of Dr. William Beanes, a Maryland physician who had been caught resisting the British in Washington. All through the night of September 13, Key and Beanes stood on the deck of the enemy ship and watched the attack on the fort about eight miles away. As Key peered through a small telescope, the doctor kept asking, "Is the flag still there?" Flashes of light from the rockets and cannons periodically illuminated the fort, revealing that the American flag still flew proudly above the ramparts. In the morning, when the British ceased the attack and the fort had not surrendered, Key was overjoyed. He used the back of a letter he had been carrying to jot down a poem describing the attack. Later in the day, he decided to make it a song, to be sung to the tune of "To Anacreon in Heaven," a popular drinking song of the day. A friend took the song to a Baltimore newspaper, which published it. Because of its patriotic content, it immediately became popular in Baltimore. Within weeks, the song's fame spread to other cities, and it became a favorite folk song. The

Francis Scott Key witnessed the British bombardment of Fort McHenry. So moved was he by the sight of the fort, still standing in the early hours of the morning, that he wrote "The Star-Spangled Banner" to commemorate the event.

song did not receive the title "The Star-Spangled Banner" until several years later. It was not until March 3, 1931, that Congress adopted it as the country's official anthem.

by the "rockets' red glare." He was so moved by the scene, he began to jot down his impressions on the back of a letter. Later, he turned those words into a poem that became the national anthem.

In the morning, the British saw that Fort McHenry had somehow endured the attack. The U.S. flag still waved proudly above the ramparts, or fortified walls, of the battered structure. Cochrane now realized that any further attempts to capture Baltimore would be useless, and he withdrew his forces. The British sailed out of Chesapeake Bay, leaving the Americans with the task of rebuilding the smoldering U.S. capital. An important part of Britain's grand invasion plan had been only partly successful.

A Country Crumbling from Within

The second part of the British three-pronged invasion plan was even less successful. On August 31, 1814, General Prevost led a large force of British troops down the length of Lake Champlain with the intention of conquering New York. He was supported by British ships on the the lake. An American fleet commanded by Lt. Thomas Macdonough moved to meet the British ships at Plattsburgh, on the western shore of the lake. On September 11, two days before the British bombardment of Fort McHenry, Macdonough defeated the British fleet. Lacking the support of his ships, Prevost ordered his army to retreat back into Canada. The Americans saw it as a major U.S. victory, while the British

Lt. Thomas Macdonough (below) defeated the British in the sea battle on Lake Champlain (bottom).

GRAND VICTORY ON LAKE CHAMPLAIN.

[TENTH NAVAL VICTORY.—" COM. MACDONOUGH obtained a glorious victory, over the British Fleet, on Lake Champlain Sept. 11. The Squadrons were nearly equal in force, and the carnage is reported to have been very great. The vessels captured were a Frigate of 32 guns, mounting 37—a Brig of 22 guns—2 Sloops of 1o guns each, and several Gallies ;—indeed the whole British force on the Lake,—3 Gallies excepted which escaped." The action lasted 2 hours 15 min.---Loss on board their Ship 1o6 men---The Growler had but 5 men left alive---their commander Downie killed at the first fire.---Our Com. Macdonough is safe !---HONOR TO THE BRAVE !---]

The Old-War Proverb still holds good ; " There's VIRTUE, in the YANKEE blood."

TUNE---" Hark ! hark ! the joyful news is come."

THE triumphs of your country sing,
  And hail the *Videttes*, as they bring,
From *North* and *South*...Good News :
Our ranks have *Heroes*...not a few,
All *British* foes they WILL subdue !
  No more shall they abuse !
Rise *PATRIOTS*, rise !...Obey your Coun-
  try's call ;
  D we all stand !...Divided *FALL* !!
  Britain's vengeful Clans,
    rojected plans,
  n to destroy ;
    terans, in train,
    om off all *Europes* main,
    try to annoy.
  IOTS, rise ! &c.
    Forces thus arrang'd,
    and from home estrang'd,
    owd around your shores ;
    resolute and base
    of dead, in every place,
    pointed cannon roars,
  PATRIOTS, rise ! &c.
    and Carnage...Ruin...all,
    ympathetic heart appal,
  And stagger our belief ;
  they swear your cities all shall flame,
To blast your *Hopes*, your *Rights*, your *Fame*
  In unavailing grief.
  Rise ! *PATRIOTS* rise ! &c.
Cities and *Villages* are fired,
Your *Nation's CAPITOL's*...not spared,
  Nor *Alexandria* sav'd ;
The *ENEMY* your strength defies,
Your brave Militia, they despise,
  With blood, your streets are pav'd !
  Rise ! *PATRIOTS* rise ! &c.
Alas ! how fills th' eventful year...
Their Troops are round our whole *frontier*,
  With *Instruments of Death* !
Their *Savage Allies* all in arms,
Thro' all our country, spread alarms,
  As rapid as their breath.
  Rise ! *PATRIOTS*, rise ! &c.
Ross was the greater *Savage* far ;
BROCK was the *Gentleman* in war,
  And lean'd to *Virtue's* side !
But *Ross and Cochrane* fruitless beast,
To make us...*Sacrifice and Cost* !
  We SPURN their daring pride.
  Rise ! *PATRIOTS*, rise ! &c.

Our troops are brave...nor yet despair ;
For all their *Threats*, we neither care ;
  Nor feel ourselves afraid :
Our vast Munitions, we retain,
We'll give them *ALL*, and draw our *Gain*,
  In th' YANKEE " mode of Trade" !
  Rise ! *PATRIOTS*, rise ! &c.
Good-News" now circulates around,
Our hearts, with grateful hopes abound,
  ...All Baltimore is *BRAVE* !
Smith, Winder, and a powerful force,
" *Repulse* the enemy with loss,"
  They...ALL their country, SAVE !
  Rise ! *PATRIOTS* rise ! &c.
But mark, kind reader, *Patriots* say,
" Rejoice triumphantly...THIS DAY,"
  The Eleventh of September ;"
A *Tenth GRAND VICTRY*, is obtain'd,
Immortal trophies you have gain'd,
  PERRY'S Compeer remember.
  Rise ! *PATRIOTS* rise ! &c.
The far-fam'd *Plattsburgh and Champlain*,
New honorary triumphs, gain,
  MACDONOUGH's Brave in War,
He leads the *New-York VETRANS* on,
Vermont unites,...the *Vic'try's* won,
  " Green Mountain boys,"...Huzza !
  Rise ! *PATRIOTS*, rise ! &c.
Sir George Prevost directs his bands,
And makes *INVASION*, on our lands,
  To multiply our fears ;
But *HE*, nor *Downie*, nor *O'Brien*,
Can " lather Yankees"...after trying,...
  We " shave close"...English Peers !
  Rise ! *PATRIOTS*, rise ! &c.
With but one *hundred* Guns *and six*,
One *hundred twenty-five*, we fix,
  In silence, most complete !
Our brave *MILITIA* stand *their* fire,
Their *FLEET's* " cut up"...their *TROOPS*
  retire,
  And *Thousands* we defeat !
  Rise ! *PATRIOTS*, rise ! &c.
Army to army...fleet to fleet,
In all their pride and spirit meet,
  In rivalry and ire ;
The *Yankees*, " in close action," move,
And to the *Enemy*, they prove...
  An opposing *wall of Fire*.
  Rise ! *PATRIOTS*, rise, &c.

Wildly the *Drum*...the *Cannons* roar,
The echoes tremble round the shore,
  Thick clouds of smoke arise ;
Clangor of arms, and shouts, and groans,
...The mingled sacrifice atones !
  ...There many a HERO dies !
Broadside and *broadside* close they run,
MACDONOUGH conquers...man for gun
  On board the *Frigate* Royal ;...
To prove true *Bravery* is ours,
To prove our *Eagle* never cowers !
  To prove our hearts are *loyal*.
  Rise ! *PATRIOTS*, rise ! &c.
" The agony is over"...THERE,
But still we pledge our hearts and swear...
  Our country to defend :
Then give us " Honorable Peace"
We're " Enemies in War," for this,
  With this...we're all...the FRIEND
  Rise *PATRIOTS*, rise, &c !
Your hopes, ye *Britons*, all are vain,
You never can the *War* maintain,
  When all OUR hearts UNITE ;
Our hearts-blood is refin'd and pure,
Nor will we *Insolence* endure,
  For RIGHTS AND LAWS,...WE
  fight !
  Rise ! *PATRIOTS* rise, ! &c.
Then cease your efforts to subdue ;
We'll yield to no pow'r ;—nor to YOU ;
  Ye vet'ran *Barb'rous* Clans ;
Withdraw your troops and send them home
Or give them *Freedom*, when they come ;
  And so change all your plans.
  Rise ! *PATRIOTS*, rise, &c.
For *Freedom* and for *Rights* contest;
Like *YANKEES*, may you then be blest,
  Beyond all other powers ;
For *US*—may all our *Blessings* be—
Enrich'd with Fame and Liberty,
  And be they always OURS.
Rise ! *PATRIOTS*, rise !---Obey your Coun-
  try's call ;
UNITED we all stand !---Divided *FALL* !
  Full Chorus.
Huzza ! Huzza ! for FREEDOM RIGHTS
  and HONOR !
Huzza ! Huzza ! for COM. M'DONOUGH.

☞ Printed by N. COVERLY.

This broadsheet from 1814 tells the tale of Macdonough's victory at Lake Champlain.

considered it only a temporary setback. The British fully expected to launch another strike from Canada at a later date.

In the meantime, the third part of the British plan, the capture of New Orleans and the southern United States, was about to begin. The British had assembled a large force of ships and troops for the operation, and they were confident of victory. For one thing, the American coast along the Gulf of Mexico was militarily the weakest part of the country. The population of the region was small, and there were few forts guarding the frontier and coastal towns.

There was another reason for the British to be confident of victory in the South. By October 1814, the U.S. government was on the verge of collapse. It was almost out of money. Thanks to the pre-war embargo and the great cost of running the war, there was no longer enough money in the Treasury to pay the existing army, much less raise more troops. Enlistments reached an all-time low. Imposing taxes to raise the needed money seemed out of the question. President Madison was highly unpopular after the fall of Washington, and confidence in the government was declining. Madison thought about initiating a draft, or ordering men into the army rather than asking for volunteers, but the New England states threatened to secede if he did so. Madison could not risk splitting the nation. With the British approaching New Orleans, some American leaders feared their nation was doomed. Just when it most needed strength and unity to beat back a foreign invader, the country was crumbling from within.

CHAPTER SEVEN

Triumph in New Orleans

M any Americans believed that New Orleans would fall to the British. There were only a few thousand U.S. troops under Andrew Jackson to defend the entire southern frontier, including the cities of Mobile and New Orleans. By December 1814, Admiral Cochrane, who had led the expedition against Washington, was ready to launch a large-scale attack on the American Gulf coast. There seemed little hope that Jackson could repel the much larger British forces. Most American congressmen were worried that a defeat in the South would be a disaster for the country. Some lawmakers stated openly that if the southern part of the country came under British control, Madison's already unpopular administration would surely topple.

Pointing a Pistol at the Nation's Heart

Madison was already in serious political trouble. Many blamed him for the poor planning that led to the shameful sacking of Washington. With practically no money in the Treasury, the president was unable to forge an effective regular army. He had earlier called for the creation of an army of more than sixty thousand men. But in the fall of 1814, only about half that number were serving in the military. Many troops were poorly equipped and supplied. And many had not been paid in months, so morale was low.

Madison also faced formidable and increasing opposition from the New England states. They had been against the war from the beginning. Now, after the burning of the capital and with defeat in the South looming, their opposition to the war became more vocal than ever. Congressmen from New England continually called on Madison to end the war by accepting whatever terms the British demanded, and they often tried to block the president's attempts to unify the country against the British.

The tensions between New Englanders and the federal government became more critical than ever in November and December 1814. The British seized about one hundred miles of Maine coastline, then part of Massachusetts. A British attack on Boston appeared imminent. Caleb Strong, the governor of Massachusetts, agreed to call out the militia but insisted that state officials must lead the troops. He also arrogantly demanded that the federal government pay for supporting his state militia. Madison staunchly refused to agree to either of these conditions.

The angry Governor Strong called a secret meeting of leaders from the New England states. The meeting, which began on December 15, 1814, in Hartford, Connecticut, became known as the Hartford Convention. The representatives discussed the possibility of seceding from the United States and making a separate peace with Britain. If they had actually done so, the rest of the country would not have been strong enough to defend itself against Britain. The British would have been victorious, and the United States would have ceased to exist.

Luckily, the more moderate members of the Hartford Convention gained control. They put aside the idea of secession for the moment. Instead, they proposed doing away with the federal army. The states would defend themselves with their own troops, using money raised within their own borders. The federal government had always objected to this idea because of the distinct danger that some states would selfishly refuse to help others who were under attack. With many separate armies and no federal control, it would be difficult or impossible to coordinate a defense against a foreign threat to the nation as a whole. But the members of the convention were more interested in states' rights than in national rights. They decided that if Congress did not go along with their demands, they would then meet again to consider seceding. Their secret plan was, in the words of one historian, like a pistol pointed "at the heart of the Union." If Madison agreed to eliminate the federal army, the national government would no longer be able to properly defend the country. If he did not give in to the convention's demands, New England would secede. Either way, the nation would suffer.

Three convention members rode from Hartford in early January to present their demands to the president. As they headed for Washington, messengers on a very different mission sped northward from New Orleans. The news they carried would overshadow the convention's demands and silence New England's opposition to the war.

Battle for New Orleans

MISSOURI TERRITORY

TENNESSEE

NORTH CAROLINA

Cumberland R.

Tennessee R.

Huntsville

Coosa R.

CREEK WAR 1813-1814

SOUTH CAROLINA

Mississippi R.

MISSISSIPPI TERRITORY

GEORGIA

Savannah R.

Charleston

Vicksburg

Alabama R.

HORSESHOE BEND

JACKSON

Savannah

Mobile

ATLANTIC OCEAN

LOUISIANA

JACKSON

Pensacola

FLORIDA

New Orleans Jan. 8, 1815

Ft. Bowyer

St. Augustine

PAKENHAM

Ft. St. Phillip

GULF OF MEXICO

SCALE OF MILES

0   50   100   150   200

BATTLES..........................

AMERICAN DRIVES........

BRITISH DRIVES.............

Jackson Prepares for Battle

New Orleans lies one thousand miles from Washington, D.C., and more than thirteen hundred miles from New England. In the early 1800s, messengers riding overland took as long as ten days to cover these distances. So, the members of the Hartford Convention did not know what had happened in the South during the Christmas and New Year's holidays of 1814 and 1815. The last news they had heard indicated that Admiral Cochrane's forces were attacking New Orleans. According to reliable reports, the British had fifty huge warships, more than ten thousand men, and at least one thousand movable cannons. This was the largest foreign army ever to move against an American city. Like most other Americans, the New Englanders assumed that any further news from New Orleans would be bad. They did not yet appreciate the talent, leadership abilities, and raw courage of Gen. Andrew Jackson.

Jackson, commanding only about two thousand troops, had arrived in New Orleans on December 1, 1814, to begin fortifying the city. He strengthened the forts surrounding the city, built barricades, and placed units of armed men at strategic points. But Jackson realized that these preparations were not enough to stop the British. He correctly reasoned that preparing the Louisiana militia and other local people was vital.

Jean Laffite and His Pirates

Jean Laffite (1780–ca. 1825) was a colorful combination of pirate, smuggler, and patriot who aided the Americans in their defense of New Orleans against the British. Nothing is known about his early life, but by 1810 he was in command of a band of smugglers based on the shore of the Baratarian Bay south of New Orleans. Laffite raided Spanish ships and sold the stolen goods on the thriving black market in New Orleans. Since he never attacked U.S. ships and helped the economy of the area, the Americans left him alone. The British realized that Laffite and his pirates could be a valuable military asset in their conquest of the American Gulf coast. In 1814, British agents offered Laffite thirty thousand dollars and a commission in the British navy if he helped them defeat the Americans. Laffite refused. He immediately sent the documents outlining the British proposal to the American authorities to warn them of the British threat. Claiming to be an American patriot, Laffite offered his services to Andrew Jackson, under the condition that the United States would later pardon the pirates for their illegal actions. Jackson, badly in need of soldiers, accepted. At the Battle of New Orleans on January 8, 1815, Laffite and his men fought with distinction, and President Madison later issued them a public pardon. In 1821, Laffite loaded up his belongings and a crew of trusted followers

Jean Laffite was a unique combination of pirate and patriot. Even though he was offered thirty thousand dollars by the British, Laffite refused to cooperate with them, claiming a loyalty to the United States.

and sailed away. He was never heard from again, and his later life remains as much of a mystery as his youth.

The forces Jackson put together were colorful. At that time, the population of Louisiana contained a broad mix of many cultures and nationalities. A majority of the people were descended from the French and Spanish who originally settled the area. There were American fur trappers and frontiersmen, Choctaw and other local Indians, and former black slaves. In addition, there were many Creoles, who were white or black people of mixed American and Spanish or French descent. In less than three weeks, Jackson organized nearly two thousand of these locals into a defensive militia. The force even included a group of pirates from the southern coast of Louisiana led by the personable Jean Laffite. The pirates, who preyed mainly on Spanish shipping, claimed to be loyal Americans and offered their services to Jackson. On December 23, Jackson's forces received a further boost when twenty-five hundred volunteers that he had earlier requested from Tennessee arrived.

The British Move Ashore

Jackson was fortunate that he was able to prepare his defenses so quickly. On the very day that the Tennesseans rode into New Orleans, the British were approaching the city. Admiral Cochrane had faced a formidable task in getting his men ashore. At that time, New Orleans was nearly surrounded by swamps and shallow rivers that his large ships could not navigate, so he had to anchor his fleet fifty miles offshore. Thousands of troops and tons of supplies had to be rowed ashore in cutters, a tedious and difficult endeavor. But Cochrane had cutters moving day and night and quickly established a base of operations on the Louisiana coast.

While Cochrane's troops continued to move ashore, Gen. John Keane led a force of more than two thousand British troops north toward New Orleans. On December 23, he captured a river plantation located about seven miles south of the city. There, he and his troops camped for the night. The overconfident Keane fully expected to take the city the next day even without the rest of the army. He knew Jackson had few regular troops, and he expected little resistance from the Indians, blacks, and Creoles. Also, Keane remembered how the Americans had run away at Bladensburg. He assured his men that the American "dirty shirts" in New Orleans were cowards who would run just as fast.

When Jackson received word of the capture of the plantation, he angrily smashed his fist into the nearest table. "By the Eternal, they shall not sleep on our soil!" he exclaimed. Acting swiftly and decisively, he summoned his officers and told them, "Gentlemen, the British are below [to the south]. We must fight them tonight."

That evening, Jackson led a force of about two thousand troops, including some two hundred free blacks and many Creoles,

Andrew Jackson—Old Hickory

Andrew Jackson (1767–1845), one of the country's most honored war heroes, became the seventh president of the United States. Born in a log cabin in South Carolina, Jackson fought in the Revolution. He was captured and suffered a sword wound when he refused to clean the boots of a British officer. Later, he settled in Tennessee, where he studied law and married a fiery young woman named Rachel Robards. She did not divorce her first husband, and Jackson threatened to fight a duel with anyone who dared to question his or Rachel's honor. In one of these duels, he killed a man. After serving in Congress, he became a judge and a major general in the Tennessee militia.

During the War of 1812, Jackson distinguished himself by leading American troops against the Creek Indians, who threatened American settlers on the southern frontier. For refusing to bend to what he considered unreasonable requests from his superiors, he earned the nickname Old Hickory. In January 1815, he led the U.S. forces that defeated the British in New Orleans, which made Jackson an instant national hero.

Jackson's fame endured and helped him win the presidency in 1828. As president, he expanded voting rights and paid off the national debt. After serving a second term, he retired in 1836 to the Hermitage, his plantation in Tennessee.

Andrew Jackson was a well-known figure during the early years of the United States and as the country expanded westward.

to within one hundred yards of the occupied plantation. Meanwhile, the American gunboat *Carolina* moved silently along a waterway on the other side of the British camp. The boat's cannons suddenly opened fire, taking Keane and his men completely by surprise. A few minutes later, Jackson's forces attacked, and there was bloody hand-to-hand combat for nearly four hours. At about midnight, Jackson reasoned that Keane would soon receive reinforcements and wisely withdrew.

In this first battle of their campaign against the southern United States, forty-six British soldiers were killed, and more than two hundred were wounded and captured. Although the American losses were almost as heavy, Jackson's quick action had given them the advantage. The British soldiers were shaken and now saw the "dirty shirts" as an enemy to be feared and respected. At the same time, Jackson's hastily trained and culturally diverse forces became more confident. They had proved that they could stand up to the British army and looked forward to driving the invaders from Louisiana.

The Battle of New Orleans

The two armies now prepared for a major confrontation. On Christmas Day in 1814, Gen. Edward Pakenham, a veteran of the war with France, replaced Keane as head of the British ground troops. Pakenham immediately moved the main body of his army northward. At the same time, Jackson ordered his own troops to make a stand along a narrow canal a few miles south of New Orleans. Because of the swamps and other natural barriers in the area, the British had to cross the canal in order to reach the city. The Americans constructed a five-foot-high dirt wall about thirty

New Orleans

The city of New Orleans was founded by the French in 1718. The settlement grew quickly because of its strategic location. Traders, fur trappers, and explorers from many nations passed through New Orleans as they traveled along the Mississippi into the vast frontier that stretched northward. In 1763, the British gained control of Louisiana, except for New Orleans, which the French gave to Spain. The Spanish ruled the city until 1800, when France once again took charge of Louisiana. When Thomas Jefferson bought the territory from France in 1803, New Orleans came under American control.

Louisiana gained official U.S. statehood in 1812. By that time, New Orleans was a flourishing trade center with imports and exports exceeding seven million dollars per year. Though an American city, it retained its mixture of cultures, which now included Indians, former black slaves, immigrants from Cuba and other Caribbean islands, and international pirates. A large percentage of the population was Creole, or mixed-race. Members of all these diverse groups united in 1814 under Andrew Jackson to meet the British invasion threat. At the Battle of New Orleans on January 8, 1815, they decisively defeated the British.

feet behind the canal. They erected wooden platforms atop the wall, placed cannons on the platforms, and protected the guns with huge cotton bales. By New Year's Eve, Pakenham had placed dozens of British cannons seven hundred yards directly in front of the American fortifications.

The next morning, January 1, 1815, Pakenham decided to attack. He planned to use his cannons to blast holes in Jackson's wall, then march his infantry through the holes. At Pakenham's signal, the expert British gunners blasted away, scoring hits on Jackson's field headquarters as well as on an American supply boat. A few minutes later, the American cannons answered, scoring their own direct hits on British positions. The opposing guns roared at each other relentlessly for 2½ hours. When it was over, Pakenham saw that the American positions were still intact. He decided to postpone the attack until he received more reinforcements from the coast.

By January 8, Pakenham felt he was finally ready to overrun the American positions. At dawn, he fired a rocket, the signal for Keane and other British commanders to move forward. The troops advanced in the open, marching in perfect formation to a beat pounded out by a long row of drummers. Without benefit of cover, long lines of redcoats headed straight toward the American guns. This impractical style of warfare had been traditional in Europe for centuries. But the Americans, as well as the British commanders in Canada, had abandoned it long ago. They

As the British charge in orderly columns, American soldiers fire cannonballs straight into their lines during the Battle of New Orleans.

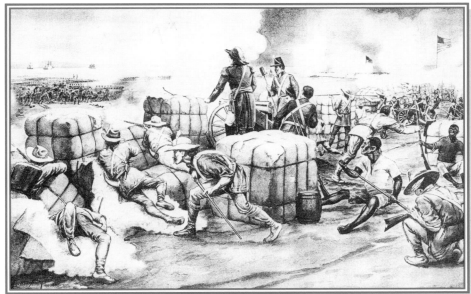

As the British advance, U.S. riflemen, under command of Andrew Jackson, alternate in rows (above) to keep up a continuous stream of musket fire. (right) American riflemen were able to defeat the British with the use of superior tactics.

considered it suicidal because the troops were helpless against enemy fire. But this was the way Pakenham had fought Napoleon, and he stuck with tradition.

The Americans watched in disbelief as the troops advanced. Countering the British drummers, U.S. flutes and drums loudly played "Yankee Doodle." When the enemy was close enough, Jackson ordered his largest cannon to discharge a load of musket balls and scrap metal. The rain of fragments tore into the British ranks, and more than two hundred men collapsed at the same time. Then, the other American cannons began to blast away, and more redcoats fell. Despite these losses, the British continued to advance in orderly, disciplined formation.

As the British came within range of the American muskets, the brilliance of Jackson's defensive plans became obvious. He had lined up his riflemen in four rows, one behind the other. After the men in the first row fired, they moved back, allowing the men in the second row to step forward. As the members of the first two

After leading charge after futile charge and being wounded twice, British General Pakenham is fatally wounded in the Battle of New Orleans.

rows reloaded, the third and fourth rows took their turns. One devastating volley after another shattered the British lines.

Pakenham had greatly underestimated the strength of Jackson's forces. But he hoped that the Americans could be overwhelmed by the sheer number of British troops. When some of his redcoats finally turned to flee, Pakenham bravely galloped into the fray and formed the men into another line. But the deadly barrage of American gunfire quickly tore this new line to pieces. Wave after wave of redcoats marched forward, only to be cut down. A handful of British soldiers managed to make it to the canal and dirt wall. None survived the lethal array of muskets, pistols, and swords that awaited them. Pakenham, wounded twice, continued to rally his men until a third American musket ball ended his life. Keane fell nearby after taking a shot through the throat. Finally, one of Pakenham's officers had the wisdom to end the slaughter by ordering a retreat. Shocked and bleeding, the surviving British soldiers crept away toward the safety of their ships.

The News of Victory

Jackson had won a victory of epic proportions. The British losses were staggering: 291 dead, 1,262 wounded, and 484 missing. By contrast, only 13 Americans were killed and 39 were wounded. Admiral Cochrane now found himself in a dangerous position. British casualties were terribly high, and the morale of the rest of the men had been shattered. The fleet was still many miles offshore and could offer no support to the land forces. The Americans would surely counterattack in full strength at any moment. There was no choice but to withdraw and abandon the expedition, which Cochrane did.

The news of the American victory in New Orleans did not reach the Northeast until well past the middle of January 1815. By that time, the three messengers from the Hartford Convention were in Baltimore. They were shocked and unsure of what to do. Jackson's triumph had greatly strengthened Madison's position, and they worried that the president might now have the support to force New England to back down. The messengers continued on to Washington, but the town was celebrating the win in the South and no one seemed interested in their demands. All over the country, people talked of little else but Jackson's victory and of U.S. victories yet to come.

But there would be no more victories. What no one in North America knew was that the war had been over for weeks. On February 13, 1815, a ship arrived from Europe with the momentous news. American and British negotiators had signed a peace treaty in the Belgian town of Ghent on Christmas Eve in 1814. This was a full two weeks before the Battle of New Orleans. Had the means of communication been quicker at the time, that bloody encounter might have been avoided. But American leaders were glad that the battle had been fought. It seemed to end a long, frustrating, and seemingly unwinnable conflict on a positive note. On February 17, 1815, President Madison officially announced that the war with Britain was over at last.

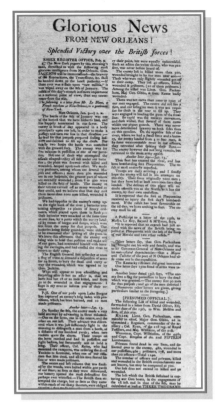

This broadside from January 8, 1815 celebrates in detail the "Glorious News from New Orleans."

The Peace That Came Too Late

The document signed at Ghent ending the War of 1812 was markedly different from most other peace treaties. Usually, one side in a conflict decisively defeats the other, or one side is unable to continue fighting. The warring parties then sit down to make peace. But when the Treaty of Ghent was signed on December 24, 1814, neither Britain nor the United States had gained complete victory. Moreover, both nations could and did continue fighting for several more weeks.

The peace talks took place, on and off, all through the war, rather than at the end of the fighting. Negotiators from the two countries met many times in both England and Belgium. They constantly argued over such issues as shipping rights, Britain's impressment of U.S. sailors, and control of Indian lands. When news of an American victory reached Europe, the U.S. negotiators bargained, for a time, with a stronger hand. Similarly, news of a British win enabled the British side to temporarily make stronger demands. As each side tried to establish a clear advantage over the other, the talks dragged on and on.

The War's Causes Ignored

What finally persuaded the negotiators to sign the treaty was the realization that for both nations, the war was unwinnable. It was expensive, and military forces had to be spread out over vast stretches of land and sea. The two countries had racked up a fairly equal number of victories and defeats. By the end of 1814, things were not going very well for either side, so each thought it best to salvage whatever it could and get out of the conflict.

This reflected a major change of attitude on the part of the British. They had been unwilling to bargain in the summer of 1814 when their invasion forces were headed for the United States. But later, their attack on New York fizzled and they were forced to retreat from Baltimore. By December, their only major hope was that Cochrane's forces would be able to capture New Orleans. This would give them control of the Louisiana Territory and a foothold in North America. The British signed the treaty confident that Cochrane was already winning. Even after the signing, they authorized sending him reinforcements to help him hold onto the new gains. The British intended to put the war behind them, and then go on to develop their new North American colony.

The Americans were also anxious to end the fighting. They had gained control of the Great Lakes and frontier areas. But the Treasury was nearly empty, and the army was not large enough to carry on a sustained war. New England was about to secede, and the government was in danger of collapse. In addition, the British were approaching New Orleans. American negotiators hoped to bring the war to a close before the British captured the southern United States and Louisiana.

So, each side had its reasons for ending the war, and the negotiators signed the treaty. They still had not, however, resolved the issues over which the war had been fought. They could not reach agreement on a single point, so they decided to temporarily ignore their mutual grievances. The Treaty of Ghent was no more than a statement that the countries would cease hostilities. There was no mention of shipping rights, impressment,

The signing of the Treaty of Ghent. Although both the British and the Americans were eager to end hostilities, the treaty did not resolve any of the issues for which the war was fought.

In this nineteenth-century engraving, the end of the War of 1812 is depicted in grand terms. Unfortunately, the war did little in terms of resolving the issues that had led to it.

Indian issues, or territorial gains for either nation. The parties stated their intentions to discuss and hopefully resolve these issues in future meetings. For the moment, the negotiators preferred to maintain what they called the *status quo ante bellum,* or "situation that existed before the war."

Restoring the Nation's Pride

Of course, as they signed the treaty, the negotiators on both sides believed that the British would likely capture Louisiana. But Andrew Jackson surprised everyone. His decisive victory quickly overshadowed the treaty itself and became, in everyone's mind, the real conclusion of the war. It was Jackson's win, not the treaty, that ended British dreams of an empire in North America. To many British, the battle was a tragic waste that might have been avoided if news of peace had not arrived so late.

In the United States, many people thought that the victory in New Orleans signaled that the Americans had won the war. The news from Louisiana spread across the country nearly a month before the word from Ghent arrived. Many people mistakenly thought that Jackson's victory had forced the British to sign the treaty. In reality, there was no clear-cut winner. At war's end, the biggest successes the United States could claim were that it had lost no territory and that its government had not collapsed.

Yet Jackson's stunning victory instilled a new sense of pride in the American people. There was a widespread feeling that they had overcome British tyranny a second time. A surge of patriotism gripped the country and brought a sense of unity that had been lacking for many years. American diplomat Albert Gallatin summed up the new national attitude: "The war has renewed…the national feelings and character which the Revolution had given…. The people…are more American; they feel and act more as a nation."

The new unity brought an end to some long-standing political squabbles. Most people now agreed that the needs of the country as a whole should come before the needs of individual states. New England's complaints and demands now seemed petty and its leaders disloyal. In contrast, respect for the federal government increased, and future presidents would find it easier to unite the country in time of danger.

Lessons in Warfare

The War of 1812 taught both the British and Americans important lessons about waging war. Britain, a world-class power, had been unable to easily subdue the far less powerful United States. This was partly because of Britain's attempt to fight the French and Americans at the same time. For most of the war, the British could not devote adequate troops and supplies to the American conflict, which gave the Americans time to expand and improve

The memory of Jackson's victory at New Orleans continued to be a source of pride for Americans after the War of 1812.

their own army. The British also assigned their best generals to the fight against Napoleon. Most of the British leaders in America lacked skill, imagination, and daring. They were also overconfident, often assuming that the Americans were undisciplined and unskilled. It was this attitude that led to Captain Dacres's loss of the *Guerriere* and General Pakenham's defeat in New Orleans.

The Americans also learned a lesson about overconfidence. The war hawks had declared war believing that invading and conquering Canada would be an easy affair. William Hull lost Detroit because he expected the British to retreat at the first sight of an American army. Fortunately, the Americans later changed their attitude. Part of what made Oliver Perry and Andrew Jackson effective leaders was their respect for the enemy's ability.

Perhaps the most important military lesson the Americans learned was to be prepared. At the outset of the fighting, the country's army was much too small to fight a major war. The troops had little training, and the generals were inexperienced. The navy lacked firepower and sufficient vessels to defend thousands of miles of coastline. After the war, the state of the military became a national priority. The country began to maintain a large, well-trained standing army and vastly increased the size of the navy. Never again would the United States be so unprepared to defend itself.

Wealth and Expansion

The War of 1812 also brought about another kind of U.S. military expansion, one that would have important consequences for the nation's future. The country developed the beginnings of a major weapons industry. Before the war, many of the arms used by U.S. troops came from other countries. But the British Orders in Council, which limited U.S. shipping, deprived the Americans of

The Americans' victories over the British navy were stunning. British overconfidence did much to add to their losses.

Westward Expansion

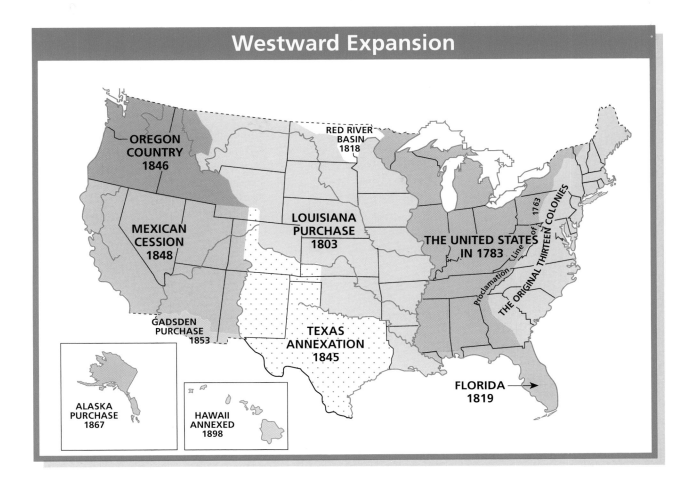

these foreign weapons. American artisans and engineers rose to the challenge. They managed to produce all the muskets, cannons, and gunpowder needed to wage the war. U.S. manufacturing plants grew in size and number, and American companies even began selling weapons to other countries. The United States has been one of the world's major arms suppliers ever since.

This increase in manufacturing greatly boosted the country's economy, which, in turn, sparked more industrial growth and helped the United States become a wealthy nation. Also adding to the country's wealth were the lands taken from the Indians during the war. White settlers' hatred for the Indians increased during the war because so many tribes were allied with the British, and killing Indians seemed more acceptable to many Americans. Many of the Creek territories seized became rich southern cotton plantations. The Indian lands of the Ohio Valley became farms, part of the vast midwestern "breadbasket" that would feed the nation's growing population. The frontier also yielded furs, timber, and precious metals.

The control of the frontier that was gained during the war also allowed the United States to begin a rapid process of westward expansion. This movement would be unstoppable, ending only when the country stretched from the Atlantic to the Pacific oceans. The expansion was driven by an aggressive attitude the American people had acquired during the war with Britain. After stopping the British from extending their empire into the vast western frontier, Americans had a new feeling of national strength and pride. Many Americans came to believe that it was their destiny to control this frontier, and they looked upon other nations and peoples holding lands in the frontier as intruders. Throughout the nineteenth century, the United States, either by war or negotiation, absorbed huge territories belonging to Spain, Mexico, France, Britain, and the American Indians. All this acquisition of wealth and territory in the 1800s helped the United States eventually become a world power.

The English-Speaking Alliance

One other important factor contributed to the United States becoming a rich and powerful nation. This factor was the friendship that developed between the Americans and the British in the decades following the War of 1812. After the war, Britain stopped seeing the United States as a country of rebels with little chance for success. The British finally accepted the United States as a permanent nation, one that could be a valuable ally and trading partner. The flourishing trade that quickly developed between the two countries greatly benefited Britain's economy and helped it maintain its huge worldwide empire. In return, Britain provided the protection of its great navy. Britain's domination of the seas ensured that no other European powers could extend their influence into North America. This guaranteed the United States a century of unlimited growth, secure from the threat of foreign intervention.

Both the Americans and the British eventually regarded the differences they had fought over as minor disputes. They signed agreements settling these disputes and began to build a positive and lasting relationship. In time, this course of events seemed only natural. The two countries had, after all, a great deal in common. They shared the same language and heritage as well as similar customs, laws, and ideas. The alliance between the two peoples would eventually help shape the course of world history. Americans and British would fight side by side defending freedom and democracy during the world wars of the twentieth century.

The most important outcome of the War of 1812 was that the warring parties quickly put their differences behind them. The Treaty of Ghent had come too late to prevent the slaughter in New Orleans. But it was a peace that would endure for centuries. There was no decisive military victor in the war. Only later did it become plain that, by becoming friends, both nations ended up winners.

Glossary

bow the front of a ship.

bowsprit the long mast protruding outward from the front of a ship.

camels raftlike devices used to lift a ship high in the water, enabling it to maneuver in extremely shallow water.

capstan a revolving cylinder that pulls in or lets out rope to which an anchor or other object is tied.

cavalry soldiers mounted on horses.

cutter a small rowboat carried aboard a larger vessel.

draft the selection of civilians from certain groups for required military service.

embargo a government order prohibiting ships from leaving or entering certain ports.

frigate a large sailing warship carrying from thirty to fifty cannons.

garrison a fort, or the soldiers defending it.

gunboat a small sailing warship usually carrying from one to five cannons.

infantry soldiers who fight on foot.

kedge to drop a heavy anchor far ahead of the ship, then manually pull the ship toward the anchor.

militia ordinary citizens who can be called up for military service at a moment's notice.

musket, or **flintlock** a primitive rifle that uses a piece of flint to produce a spark, which ignites gunpowder, creating an explosion that forces a metal ball out the barrel of the weapon.

port the left side of a ship.

rake to sail in front of an enemy's ship, firing cannons and guns while passing by.

ramparts fortified walls.

ship of the line a large sailing warship carrying from fifty to eighty or more cannons.

sloop a small sailing ship with one mast and usually two sails.

squadron a group of ships.

stern the rear of a ship.

weather gauge an advantageous position during a naval encounter in which the wind carries one's ship toward the enemy's rear.

For Further Reading

Henry E. Gruppe and the editors of Time-Life Books, *The Frigates*. Alexandria, VA: Time-Life Books, 1979.

Clara Ingram Judson, *Andrew Jackson*. Chicago: Follett Publishing, 1954.

Clara Ingram Judson, *Thomas Jefferson*. Chicago: Follett Publishing, 1952.

Albert Marrin, *1812: The War Nobody Won*. New York: Macmillan, 1985.

Tyrone G. Martin, *The Most Fortunate Ship: A Narrative History of "Old Ironsides."* Chester, CT: The Globe Pequot Press, 1980.

Dave Richard Palmer and James W. Stryker, *Early American Wars and Military Institutions*. Wayne, NJ: Avery Publishing Group, 1986.

Robert Tallant, *The Pirate Lafitte and the Battle of New Orleans*. New York: Random House, 1951.

Works Consulted

Pierre Berton, *The Invasion of Canada: 1812-1813*. New York: Penguin Books, 1988.

Allan W. Eckert, *The Frontiersmen: A Narrative*. Boston: Little, Brown, 1967.

C. S. Forester, *The Age of Fighting Sail: The Story of the Naval War of 1812*. Garden City, NY: Doubleday, 1956.

Reginald Horsman, *The War of 1812*. New York: Knopf, 1969.

Dudley W. Knox, *A History of the United States Navy*. New York: G. P. Putnam's Sons, 1936.

Robert Leckie, *The Wars of America*. New York: Harper & Row, 1968.

Walter Lord, *The Dawn's Early Light*. New York: W. W. Norton, 1972.

Dumas Malone, *Jefferson the President: First Term, 1801-1805*. Boston: Little, Brown, 1970.

Dumas Malone, *Jefferson the President: Second Term, 1805-1809*. Boston: Little, Brown, 1974.

Geofferey Perret, *A Country Made by War: From the Revolution to Vietnam—The Story of America's Rise to Power*. New York: Random House, 1989.

Robert V. Remini, *Andrew Jackson and the Course of American Empire: 1767-1821*. New York: Harper & Row, 1977.

John Snyder, *Tecumseh's Last Stand*. Norman: University of Oklahoma Press, 1990.

George Rogers Taylor, ed., *The War of 1812: Past Justifications and Present Interpretations*. Boston: D. C. Heath, 1963.

Irwin Unger, *These United States: The Questions of Our Past. Vol. I, to 1877*. Boston: Little, Brown, 1978.

Index

Photo Credits

Cover picture by Library of Congress

The Bettmann Archive, 31, 71, 92

Daughters of the Republic of Texas Library, 32, 74 (both)

Illinois State Historical Society, 33, 65

Library of Congress, 8, 10, 13 (both), 14, 15 (both), 16, 18, 20, 21 (top), 22, 26 (top), 27, 30, 40, 41, 43, 44, 46, 48, 49 (both), 56, 59, 61 (both), 62, 69, 70, 73, 76, 80, 82, 84, 85, 86 (both), 87, 88, 94, 95, 96, 97 (both), 98, 99, 102

National Archives, 39, 50, 60, 81, 83 (both), 95, 101, 103, 104

National Portrait Gallery, Smithsonian Institution, 17, 21 (bottom), 23, 26 (bottom), 58, 67, 72

About the Author

Don Nardo is an actor, film director, and composer, as well as an award-winning writer. As an actor, he has appeared in more than fifty stage productions. He has also worked before or behind the camera in twenty films. Several of his musical compositions, including a young person's version of *The War of the Worlds* and the oratorio *Richard III,* have been performed by regional orchestras. Mr. Nardo's writing credits include short stories, articles, and more than twenty-five books, including *Lasers: Humanity's Magic Light; Anxiety and Phobias; The Irish Potato Famine; Exercise; Gravity: The Universal Force;* and *The Mexican-American War.* Among his other writings are an episode of ABC's "Spenser: For Hire" and numerous screenplays. Mr. Nardo lives with his wife, Christine, on Cape Cod, Massachusetts.